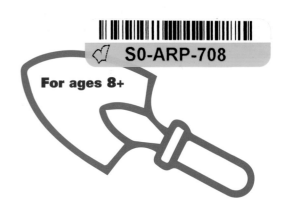

STANLEY® Jr.

GARDENING
IS AWESOME!

Brimming with creative inspiration, how-to projects, and useful information to enrich your everyday life, Quarto Knows is a favorite destination for those pursuing their interests and passions. Visit our site and dig deeper with our books into your area of interest: Quarto Creates, Quarto Cooks, Quarto Homes, Quarto Lives, Quarto Drives, Quarto Explores, Quarto Gifts, or Quarto Kids.

First Published in 2021 by Cool Springs Press, an imprint of The Quarto Group, 100 Cummings Center, Suite 265-D, Beverly, MA 01915, USA.
T (978) 282-9590 F (978) 283-2742 QuartoKnows.com

Cool Springs Press titles are also available at discount for retail, wholesale, promotional, and bulk purchase. For details, contact the Special Sales Manager by email at specialsales@quarto.com or by mail at The Quarto Group, Attn: Special Sales Manager, 100 Cummings Center, Suite 265-D, Beverly, MA 01915, USA.

25 24 23 22 21   1 2 3 4 5

ISBN: 978-0-7603-6842-8

Digital edition published in 2021

Library of Congress Cataloging-in-Publication Data available.

Design: The Quarto Group
Cover Images: Dave Brown Images and Shutterstock
Page Layout: Megan Jones Design
Photography: Dave Brown Images
Illustration: Len Churchill and Mattie Wells
   Additional photography and illustration: Shutterstock on pages 4, 6, 7, 12, 13, 17, 20, 22, 23, 29, 31, 33, 34, 36–45, 53–57, 60–63, 66, 67, 72, 75, 79, 80–82, 86, 87, 100, 107

Printed in China

Created by: The Editors of Cool Springs Press, in cooperation with STANLEY Tools.

STANLEY Tools and the STANLEY logo are trademarks of The Black & Decker Corporation and are used under license. All rights reserved.

NOTICE TO READERS

For safety, use caution, care, and good judgment when following the procedures described in this book. The publisher and STANLEY Tools cannot assume responsibility for any damage to property or injury to persons as a result of misuse of the information provided. The techniques shown in this book are general techniques for various applications. In some instances, additional techniques not shown in this book may be required. Always follow manufacturers' instructions included with products, since deviating from the directions may void warranties. The projects in this book vary widely as to skill levels required: some may not be appropriate for all do-it-yourselfers, and some may require professional help.

Consult your local building department for information on building permits, codes, and other laws as they apply to your project.

STANLEY® Jr.

GARDENING
IS AWESOME!

Projects, Advice & Insight for Young Gardeners

CHRIS PETERSON

COOL
SPRINGS
PRESS

CONTENTS

INTRODUCTION

Wouldn't it be great to have a big place to call your own, a place full of fun and adventure? Somewhere you could enjoy bright sunshine, be supercreative, do work that feels like play, and learn important things in fun ways? Well, guess what? That place is right outside your back door (or side door or front door). Whether you have a small yard, a grassy field, or a tiny concrete patio, you can grow an incredible garden full of wonderful plants that tickle your imagination, provide something delicious to eat, and impress friends and family.

Gardening is easy. You don't need to be an expert to grow a garden full of fresh herbs or delicious vegetables. Maybe you've never gardened before. That doesn't matter; you can still grow a bed of flowers or other plants. That's because plants love to grow. With a little attention and the right gardening know-how, you'll be ready to create your own dream garden.

It might be a veggie garden growing the healthiest, most delicious food there is. Or maybe you're imagining your mom's smile when you surprise her with a pot full of her favorite

A pretty, lush garden bed like this one isn't hard to create; it's just a matter of the right know-how and spending a little time making a design.

Vegetable gardens are as fun to grow as they are to eat.

flowers, blooming right outside the back door. Most important of all, when you grow a garden, you help the environment.

The right garden can even teach you all kinds of lessons—from chemistry, to biology, to math—in interesting and real-world ways that are a lot less boring than classroom lessons. That's right: your garden can make you smarter! Who knew you could "grow" better grades?

Start by understanding the conditions plants need to survive and thrive. Figure out your local seasons and weather, investigate the soil in your yard, and maybe "amend" it. How much water do your plants need? What about air circulation and pests? You'll find those answers in the first three chapters of this book.

The last three chapters are all about different types of gardens where you can put your new knowledge to work. Along the way, you'll find lots of projects, experiments, and explanations about the science of gardening. Those are superfun ways to learn and see your garden in a different light. All you'll need from then on is a little bit of good soil, some basic tools, a touch of sunlight, and a sprinkle of water every day or so. Your garden itself will supply the food, flowers . . . and the fun!

1 GARDEN ESSENTIALS

When you stand in front of a rack of seed packets or leaf through a nursery catalog, it's easy to get excited for what you can grow in your garden. There are so many different plants to choose from! Of course, plants cost money and gardening takes time and effort, so it's only smart to do a little homework and know everything you can about your garden and how it will serve your plants *before* you start gardening. That way, you won't waste time or (your parents') money.

Just like every person must have water, oxygen, food, and sleep, every plant has certain basic requirements. These include the right amounts of sunlight, water, circulating air, and nutrients. Too little, and the plant won't grow. Too much, and it's likely to die.

That's what this chapter is all about—plant basics. We start out with the most basic information of all: what is a plant? Once you understand the physical parts that almost all plants share, it's easier to grasp how plants get nutrients from soil and take up water to stay hydrated. Knowing these simple basics is the secret to growing a garden that not only survives, but really thrives and provides all the flowers or edibles you hope it will.

Once you've got these basics down, you'll get to put those seed catalogs or seed packets to good use. The choice is actually kind of simple: pretty things or things you can eat (though there is a lot of crossover between the two). You'll find loads of options from chapter 2 on, along with all the information you'll need to grow a garden in the ground, in containers, or even in raised beds that let you control everything (and make it easier to tend plants). First, though, let's cover the basics.

QUESTIONS THIS CHAPTER ANSWERS

- What is a plant?
- What is the difference between an annual and a perennial?
- What is the difference between weather and climate?
- What is a "zone"?
- How do you determine your garden's sun exposure?
- What are the types of soil?
- What are the most important soil nutrients?
- How do you determine how well your soil drains?

WHAT IS A PLANT?

Look around at all the plants in the world and they seem really different. But most of them share certain physical features that help them get nutrients and water, defend themselves against attack, and "breathe." Knowing what these features do is your first step in giving your plants exactly what they need to grow big and reward you with plump, delicious tomatoes or huge, showy flowers. Here's an easy lesson covering the most common plant parts and how they work.

ROOTS

Roots normally grow underground, although some plants, such as ivy, may have exposed roots. Roots are food and water straws for plants; it's how a plant gets hold of the building-block nutrients it uses to make its own food and the moisture it needs to maintain the cells in the plant. Some plants, such as beets and potatoes, are actually roots themselves. Most, though, have a long, sturdy *taproot*, and thin and scraggly *fibrous* roots coming off the taproot. Roots also help hold a plant in place; no plant wants to get blown over by a stiff wind.

STEMS

The stem is the "body" of a plant. Unlike our bodies, some plants have floppy and sprawling stems (such as zucchini or pumpkins), while others stand up straight and tall (such as corn). That means stems create the look of a plant and determine how much space it needs to grow. Stems are also the "highway" for a plant to transport the water and sugar that are so crucial for plants to survive and grow.

LEAVES

Leaves are the lab where *photosynthesis* occurs. That's when leaves combine water and nutrients with sunlight and carbon dioxide to make the special type of sugar that plants eat. The surface of the leaves determines how much carbon dioxide the plant can take in. It's why a tall tree with thousands of leaves can absorb so much more carbon dioxide than a mowed lawn. That's also why trees are so important for fighting climate change and greenhouse gases. Plant leaves respirate—or breathe out—an important byproduct of photosynthesis: oxygen.

FLOWERS

You might think flowers are just pretty decorations that make plants look nice. Think again! Flowers are one of the ways plants reproduce. The beautiful colors and shapes attract pollinators, which spread pollen between plants, fertilizing them. Flowers often include an *ovary*. Once fertilized, that ovary can grow into a fruit. Flowers also often contain seeds. Ever seen a dandelion flower blow apart? You're watching the seeds spread far and wide, to grow more dandelions. And here's a fun fact: some flowers are edible! Cooks include these in salads and even on desserts.

Anatomy of a Plant

Plants may not have the type of body you have, but they do have an anatomy. Their parts help them make their own food, draw water from the soil, and grow big and strong.

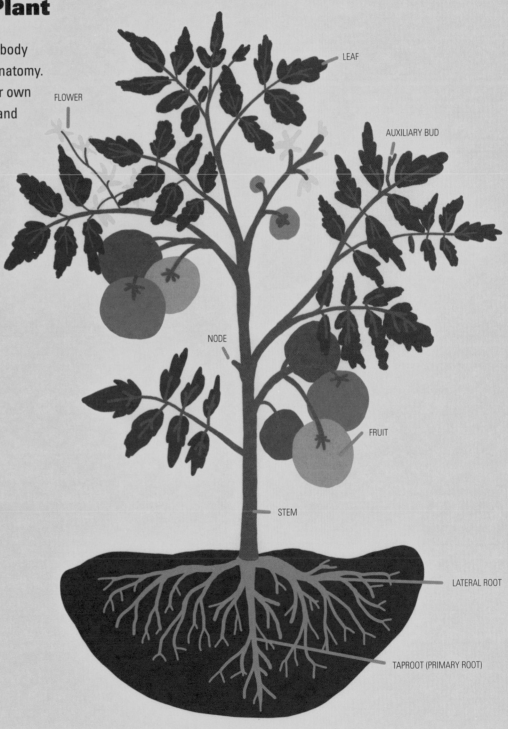

FLOWER

LEAF

AUXILIARY BUD

NODE

FRUIT

STEM

LATERAL ROOT

TAPROOT (PRIMARY ROOT)

PLANT LIFESPANS

Some plants only live for one season and then die. Those are called *annuals*. Others may lose their leaves or go dormant, but they will grow again year after year. Those are called *perennials*. A few plants only bloom, produce fruit, or live for two years. Those are called *biennials*.

PLANT NEEDS

Plants differ from animals in more ways than just their physical features. One of the biggest differences is how they eat. Obviously, plants can't raid the kitchen or hunt when they get hungry. That's why they make their own food. Yep, plants are their own kitchens. You'll hear gardeners and other people talking about "feeding" their plants, but what they really mean is that they are supplying the raw materials so that the plants can produce their own food. Plants do this through the process of photosynthesis. Fortunately for them, the raw ingredients they need for that process are the most abundant on our planet—water, sunlight, and carbon dioxide.

Plants also have to drink, just like us. Some plants are capable of taking in moisture through their leaves, but the majority of water that a plant gets will be drawn through its roots. These roots are also where plants draw in other nutrients from soil—like potassium and magnesium—that help keep the plants healthy and enable them to grow and do other functions.

THE MAGIC OF PHOTOSYNTHESIS

Photosynthesis is a basic process, but it's one that is essential to all life on Earth. Here's how it works: *Chlorophyll* traps sunlight "photons" that enter the cells of the plant as the plant is exposed to the Sun. (Chlorophyll is the compound that makes plant leaves green.) Water molecules are made up of two atoms of hydrogen and one of oxygen. The trapped photons "split" the water molecules in a plant's cells into oxygen and hydrogen. Special cells on a plant's leaves release the oxygen and take in carbon dioxide. The carbon dioxide combines with the hydrogen to create a special kind of sugar that the plant can break down for energy. That energy allows a plant to grow and function.

GARDEN JARGON

Although photosynthesis is vitally important for plant life to survive, the byproduct of this process—namely, oxygen—is responsible for Earth's human-friendly atmosphere. Put simply, plants breathe in carbon dioxide that needs to be removed from the atmosphere and breathe out oxygen, which humans need to live. This process of breathing and breaking down components for energy is called *aerobic respiration*.

UNDERSTANDING CLIMATE AND WEATHER

You might think climate and weather are the same thing, but they're not. "Weather" describes the conditions day to day. One day might be rainy, while the next is hot and sunny. Climate describes long-term trends and what happens over the course of a year in any location. You check the weather report to know if your plants are going to get a lot of rain this week. You understand your local climate so you'll know when the seasons in your region are supposed to change and to plan your growing season.

CONSIDER THE SEASONS

Seasons can be extremely different from one location to the another. Here's a breakdown of what to consider about the changing seasons no matter where you live.

Spring is when the weather turns nicer and new garden growth begins. Spring begins on the last "frost date" in your area. After that date, freezing temperatures that could kill new plants are no longer a threat.

Summer is fun! That's when most of the growth in your garden happens, and when you'll get a chance to pick your flowers and harvest fruits and vegetables. But here, again, summer is shorter or longer depending on where you live.

Autumn is often a time when the garden is shutting down. But in warmer places there is still plenty of good gardening. You can harvest seeds and, if you experience a mild autumn in your area, you may even get the chance to plant something new.

Winter is the time to clean up the garden and plan next year's harvest in most places. It's a good time to look through catalogs, read gardening books and magazines, and come up with ideas for what you'll grow starting in the spring.

MINDING MICROCLIMATES

Depending on exactly where you live, your garden may be subject to a microclimate. These are climates particular to a small area, and often noticeably different than the surrounding region. For example, inner-city gardens may be significantly warmer than yards in outlying areas. If a plant doesn't grow as well as you had hoped, consider the effect of any local microclimate.

The climate in your area will determine how soon you can plant seeds or seedlings, and will have an impact on whether those plants thrive.

SUNLIGHT & YOUR PLANTS

What Is Sunshine?

The human eye only sees a certain amount of light (what is known as the *visible spectrum*). The light we see is far from all the light there is. In fact, our eyes can only detect about 50 percent of the light rays in sunlight. That's because different types of light travel at different wavelengths. Wavelengths are measured in nanometers (nm). The human eye isn't supersensitive, so it can only read some frequencies, those between 400 to 760 nm.

Sunlight includes three types of ultraviolet (UV) rays, none of which the human eye can see. UV-C rays don't penetrate past the Earth's atmosphere. UV-A rays are the most abundant in sunlight and penetrate deeper into your skin than other UV rays. UV-B rays only affect the top layers of skin (but they're important because your body uses them to make essential Vitamin D). Both UV-A and UV-B rays accelerate skin aging and can contribute to skin diseases including cancer. Sunlight also contains *infrared light*, including Infrared-A and Infrared-B rays.

As you now know, sunlight is a critical for plants to produce the food they need to grow. Different plants prefer different amounts of sunshine—what gardeners call *sun exposure*—but all plants need some sunlight. The secret is that sunlight is not quite as simple as it looks. It contains different types of powerful ultraviolet (UV) rays. Plants absorb those rays in their leaves and use them to start the process of photosynthesis.

If you've ever had a sunburn, you know that the sun's UV rays can damage living cells. That's true of plants, as well. But here's a surprising fact: plants can essentially make their own sunscreen. Researchers in 2011 found a special UV receptor in plants. When UV-B (the most damaging of UV rays) hits a plant, it modifies a protein in that receptor, causing other cells to produce a chemical sunscreen that absorbs the UV-B rays before they can damage the plant!

That's the science. As a gardener, though, you'll deal more with the basics of sun exposure—direct sun, partial sun, or full shade. Plants fall into one of these three categories depending on well they handle the intensity of UV rays. Success in growing a garden relies on locating plants where they'll get the exposure they prefer. That means you have to know how much sun different spots in your garden receive over the course of a typical day. Most homeowners and many gardeners misjudge how much sun different areas receive. Want to be a smart gardener? Take a little time to draw up a simple sun map (see opposite).

MAPPING GARDEN SUN EXPOSURE

Saturdays and Sundays are usually good times to draw your sun map because you can be at home for the whole day. Start with a clean sheet of sketch paper, a ruler, a sharp pencil, and a set of colored pencils. Measure the yard or the area where you want to plant your garden. Make a rough scale outline of the area on the paper (usually a ratio of 1 foot (30 cm) to 1 inch (2.5 cm) works great). Sketch big features such as pathways, large trees and bushes, and sheds or other buildings.

Check the yard every hour and note the position of the sunlight in the yard as it moves through the sky. Draw yellow lines—labeling each with the time of day—and adding lines to show the borders of where the sunlight falls at different times. Do the same with areas of deep shade. At the end, you'll have all the exposure information you need to plan and plant a bang-up garden that grows exactly as it should.

As all an alternative for one garden bed or border, use a smart phone or digital camera instead of drawing a map. Take the same picture of the area from the same spot, every hour throughout the day until sunset. Looking at the photos in sequence will give you an excellent idea of how much direct sun any one area gets over time.

SAFETY FIRST!

Plants love sunshine. Humans, too. Unfortunately, it's not as healthy for you as it for your plants. It can be easy to spend an hour in your garden before you even know it. That's why it is important that you use proper sunscreen anytime you're out in the garden. Use one labeled "SPF-30" or higher. Apply it twenty minutes before you go outside and reapply it after you've been thirty minutes outside. It's also smart to wear a hat in direct sun because along with damaging your skin, harsh sunlight can dehydrate you and make you feel sick (a condition called "sunstroke").

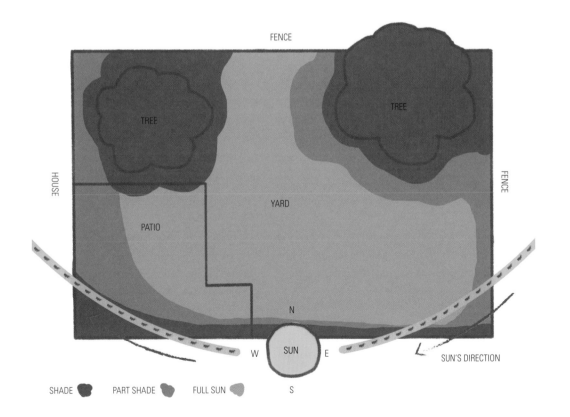

FENCE

TREE

TREE

HOUSE

FENCE

YARD

PATIO

N

W SUN E

SUN'S DIRECTION

S

SHADE   PART SHADE   FULL SUN

SOIL: THE TREASURE UNDERFOOT

Even experienced gardeners are sometimes confused about what soil is and is not. That's a shame, because making sure that the soil in your garden is as healthy as possible is key to growing the best garden you can. At the very least, you should have a good grasp of what type of soil you have, and how to improve it if necessary.

SOIL'S BIG THREE

Healthy soil contains many minerals and elements, but nitrogen, phosphorus, and potassium are the most important to the gardener. You'll see these listed on bags of fertilizer or amendments such as composted manure. They are abbreviated "N-P-K" and the percentage by volume is listed as three numbers in that order.

Nitrogen (N): Abundant in most soil, nitrogen is important because it's a key component of the amino acids that go into building proteins. Proteins keep plant cells strong, preventing a plant from withering and helping it to grow. Nitrogen is also crucial in producing chlorophyll. Chlorophyll is critical for photosynthesis.

Phosphorus (P): Think of this element as a package into which sunlight puts its energy to transfer it to a plant. Phosphorus plays a big role in helping plants convert nutrients to the building blocks plants use to grow. Phosphorus is important in establishing strong roots and helping a plant stay healthy as it ages.

Potassium (K): Although not as abundant as the other two, potassium is just as essential. This mineral increases a plant's ability to fight off diseases and helps a plant move sugars and other components to where they need to be in the plant. More importantly, it's crucial in how a plant takes in carbon dioxide.

These compounds aside, soil is made of many elements but there's not as much of it as you might think. What we call "soil" is the top layer of the Earth's surface. It's a very thin, very important layer. Soil is made up of crushed rock and living and dead plant and animal matter (called "organic matter"), which mixes with the rock or inorganic matter. Soil supplies the food and water that garden plants so badly need, and anchors plants in place. It also contains pockets of air, which allow roots to expand and grow, and a lot of beneficial microorganisms—most too small to see.

It's actually alive in a sense. That's why keeping your soil healthy is good for your garden, good for the climate, and good for the world. The question is, how do you keep soil healthy?

The answer is, by doing as little as possible to it. Soil will naturally find a healthy balance. Once upon a time, gardeners thought they had to dig up their garden plots, turning over soil 6 (15 cm), 7 (17 cm), or even 12 inches (30 cm) deep. We now know that is a bad idea. When you dig up soil—especially when you dig deep—it dries out. Beneficial organisms can die, and other bad things can happen.

The same is true if you add a lot of harsh chemicals to the soil. Even if you have the right idea—like using a chemical fertilizer to help plants grow or spraying pesticides to kill the pests that feed on your garden plants—chemicals have a way of infiltrating the soil and staying there. They kill good insects as well as bad ones, and they aren't something you want in any food you grow. Chemical additives may be easy and quick to use but adding natural amendments such as compost tea is the best way to create a vibrant healthy soil. And a healthy soil is the best way to ensure your plants grow as big and robust as possible.

You can tell rich loam just by feeling it. It crumbles easily yet you can squeeze it into a ball. It's also darker than other types of soil.

SOIL TYPES

Soil is made up of many different elements. A gardener's soil, though, can be defined by the amount of three main ingredients: sand, loam, and clay. A balanced, rich loam with small amounts of clay and sand is best for most garden plants. Unfortunately, depending on where you live, you may have an abundance of one and not enough of the others. (That's another reason gardeners sometimes "amend" the soil by adding ingredients.) In addition to the three main types described here, you may read or hear the word "silt" being called a fourth type. Silt is the nutritious organic material deposited along the shores of rivers and other bodies of water. It's not in all soils, but it's a great component.

Sand: There's a reason why few things grow on the beach. You might have seen for yourself when you play in the sand at the ocean that water flows right through this material. So do nutrients. Sand just doesn't hold together very well. Pick up a handful and it will flow through your fingers. That means sandy soil allows moisture and nutrients to pass through quickly. That's not good for plant roots because they don't get a chance to absorb those vital components. Sandy soils also don't offer a stable structure that roots can hold firm to.

Clay: Clay soils are just about the opposite of sandy soils. You have probably worked with clay in an art class and know that it sticks to itself and clumps really well. So well, in fact, that water and nutrients have a hard time getting into the soil. The thick, sticky texture of clay means that plant roots have a hard time growing and spreading.

Loam: This is the ideal soil for gardening. It contains a blend of silt, sand, and clay and many differently sized particles. That means that the soil will be workable and will allow air and water to reach plant roots. It is also substantial enough to hold moisture and nutrients and provide a firm foundation for roots. The ideal loam for the home gardener is about 40 percent silt, 40 percent sand, and 20 percent clay.

Soil's Amazing Structure

The soil we garden in is only one layer in a complicated hierarchy of soil. In fact, scientifically speaking, we garden in an incredibly thin layer at the top of several. These layers are called "horizons" (if you were to cut away a big slice of the ground, the different layers would look like horizons from the side!). Each has a different composition.

Humus: In some areas, possibly including your yard and garden, there is a thin layer of what is known as humus. Called the "organic horizon" (O), this is made up of rotting plant matter.

Topsoil: The second layer down is called the topsoil (A). It's a combination of decomposed organic matter and crushed rock that makes its way up from the layers below. This is where the roots of your garden plants take hold.

Eluviated layer: The "eluviated horizon" (E) is not present in all areas, and geologists often classify this layer as part of the subsoil—your science teacher may not count it as part of the soil structure. It is a concentrated layer of fine sand, quartz, and silt.

Subsoil: Scientists call this horizon . . . subsoil (B). It's a layer of heavier minerals that have washed down from the upper layers.

Parent material: When you realize that the top layer of soil includes a lot of decomposed rock, you can understand why this layer—composed of larger rocky particles—is called the parent material (C). It's where the tiny rock particles in topsoil began their slow, slow journey to the surface.

Bedrock: The thickest layer is the foundation for all the rest and has to hold up to crushing weight. The bedrock (R) is solid rock, although the type of rock differs from location to location. It might be granite, limestone, basalt, or another type. This layer is often dug out—mined—for its beautiful, durable stone.

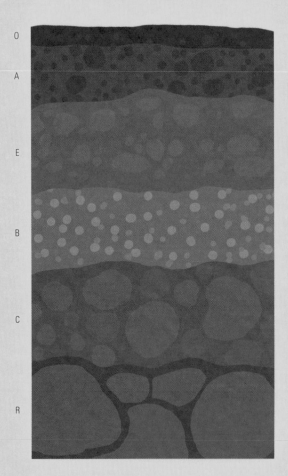

HOW TO DETERMINE YOUR SOIL TYPE

Want to discover just what kind of soil you have in your garden? Try this easy test.

WHAT YOU'LL NEED

CLEAN, EMPTY QUART MASON JAR OR 2-LITER CLEAR SODA BOTTLE

TROWEL

1 Use a trowel to scoop in enough dirt from your garden to fill the jar almost halfway. *Note: You can use a little bit of soil from different areas of your yard or garden to get a snapshot of all the soil, or you can perform several tests for different areas of the yard (the soil in a single yard or garden usually doesn't vary much).*

2 Slowly fill the jar almost to the top with clean water. Leave a little room at the top to allow you to shake up the ingredients. Tighten the lid onto the jar.

3 Shake the jar vigorously, until you're sure the water and soil have been thoroughly blended. Set the jar on a level surface where it won't be disturbed.

4 Wait four hours and then check the jar. The ingredients in the soil should have separated: sand will sink to the bottom, silt will sit on top of the sand, and clay will settle on top of the silt. Looking at the layers, what percentage of each comprises your soil? What do you think that means for drainage and nutrients in the soil?

WHAT IS SOIL ACIDITY?

Acidity is another important piece in the soil puzzle. Soil acidity is measured in terms of pH, a scale of numbers that tells you just how acidic or *alkaline* (the opposite of acidic) the soil is. Many gardeners don't think about the acidity of their soil, but it's easy to test and can be the difference between whether plants grow like crazy or barely at all.

Soil acidity is measured on a 14-point scale. Generally the best soil for most plants will be around neutral, or from 6.5 to 8 on the scale. The closer the number is to 14, the more alkaline the soil is; the closer it is to 0, the more acidic it is. Many plants, such as azaleas or blueberries, thrive in acidic soil to a level of 4, but almost none like alkaline soil (although several plants can survive in it).

Simple soil acidity test kits are available at home improvement centers, garden nurseries, and hardware stores. You just dig out a little soil from 4 inches (10 cm) below the surface and add a little bit to the test container along with distilled water and the testing medium that comes with the kit. Shake it vigorously, wait an hour, and then read the results. Once you test your soil, you'll be able to change the acidity using the right amendment (see page 24).

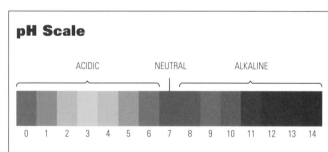

pH Scale

ACIDIC   NEUTRAL   ALKALINE

0 1 2 3 4 5 6 7 8 9 10 11 12 13 14

The pH scale is a simple scale that tells you at a glance just how acidic (or not) your soil is.

Soil acidity test kits are widely available at hardware stores, garden nurseries, and home improvement centers. The best part is that they are supereasy to use.

The Home Soil Acidity Test

It may not be as a precise as a store-bought pH test kit, but you can perform a simple experiment using a few kitchen ingredients to determine whether your soil falls on the acidic or alkaline side of the scale. You'll need plain white vinegar and baking soda.

Scoop some soil into two clear plastic containers. Add about ½ cup (120 ml) white vinegar to one and watch for a fizzing reaction. If it happens, that's the acid in the vinegar reacting to alkaline soil. Your soil is on the alkaline side. If you don't see any reaction, move on to the second sample.

Add as much water as there is soil, and then dump in ½ cup (90 gm) baking soda. Again, watch for fizzing action. If you see activity, that means the alkaline baking soda is reacting with acidic soil. Your soil is on the acidic side.

If no reaction happens in either case, you can be pretty confident that your soil has a balanced pH—just right for most garden plants!

WHAT ARE SOIL AMENDMENTS?

Not all garden soil is created equal. Depending on where you live, the soil in your backyard may be lacking in some soil essentials. For instance, people in many parts of the South deal with clay soils that don't drain well. In some parts of the Northeast, the soil is too acidic for many garden plants. The good news is, if your soil has a problem like this, you can fix it!

The cure for less-than-perfect soil is to "amend" it. That just means adding something to make the soil better. There are both natural and synthetic soil amendments. "Organic" amendments and fertilizers don't contain any synthetic chemicals that might put the soil out of balance; they fix any soil problem naturally and are longer-lasting than their artificial counterparts. For specific instructions on how to amend your soil, see page 24.

WATER WORKS

Plants are a little fussy when it comes to water. They need enough to stay hydrated, but too much will cause major problems such as root rot and can even kill a plant. That's because water serves several functions in a plant. It helps keep them cool in direct sun, and it plays a key role in helping a plant transport minerals and the sugars it needs for energy everywhere they need to go in the plant. Water is even one of the important triggers that cause a seed to germinate and grow.

Any gardener has to find a good balance with smart watering practices that keep plants growing as healthy and robust as possible. That means watering enough to keep the soil moist and your plants happy but not so much that the ground is soggy.

Unfortunately, it's all too easy to drown plants without even realizing it. An excess of water can prevent roots from getting proper nutrients and carbon dioxide from the soil and will cause a plant's survival mechanisms to malfunction. The best way to ensure that your garden plants are getting exactly the amount of water they need is to regularly check the plants in your garden for signs that they are getting too little or too much water. Once you know what to look for, the signs are pretty obvious.

WATERING OPTIONS

There are many different ways to water a garden. Regardless of the one you choose, you should aim to keep the soil lightly moist, but not saturated. Be aware that if weather turns very hot, you'll need to water more and more frequently (and, obviously, less if a sudden rainy period occurs).

No matter how you water your plants, you'll have to coordinate with natural sources of moisture to ensure that the garden isn't getting too much or too little water over time.

GARDEN JARGON

Plants have a unique way of consuming the water they need. The process is called *transpiration* and starts with the leaves of the plant drying out through wind and heat. You've seen how a dry sponge put in water will immediately soak up the water until it's saturated; that's what happens with a plant. Water is drawn up through the roots by what's known as a *capillary action* (like the sponge) and makes its way through a plant, up to the dried-out leaves.

By hand: If you are willing to be disciplined about it, you can water a garden bed with a hose or keep container plants happy with a watering can. The problem with watering by hand is that it's easy to be inconsistent and miss an area of the garden or let three or four days go by without watering. Watering has to be consistent to ensure plant health. Hand-watering is best limited to container gardens, individual pots, and single-specimen plants.

Drip line: A drip-irrigation system is a little bit of work at first, but then it eliminates just about any work on your part later on. It is a "set-it-and-forget-it" system. The most basic drip-irrigation system attaches right to the nearest hose bib with a timer and/or pressure regulator, then a filter, and then the drip tubing with emitters that water individual plants. It's not hard to set up a drip system, although you'll probably want your mom or dad to help you (and to pay for the equipment!).

Sprinklers: Some gardeners use sprinklers to keep their in-ground plants from going thirsty (sprinklers aren't usually used for container gardens). There are several different types of sprinklers, but the best for the home garden are spot sprinklers that water a small area at a time. Even though these have to be moved often to water a larger garden, they give you a lot of control over how much water goes where.

Drip line

HOW TO TEST GARDEN SOIL DRAINAGE

Before you can give your plants exactly the moisture they need, it helps to know how long it takes for water to drain through your soil. This simple test is the easiest way to determine if your garden's soil drainage needs to be improved.

TOOLS & MATERIALS

MEASURING TAPE

GARDEN SPADE OR SHOVEL

1 Dig a hole at least 12 inches (30 cm) in diameter and 12 inches (30 cm) deep. Fill the hole with water and allow it to drain completely. This will "prime" the soil for the test. Once the hole has drained (which may take overnight), refill the hole with water.

2

2 Set a 2 × 4 across the mouth of the hole. Push it firmly into the soil. Use a measuring tape to note the distance from the bottom of the hole to the bottom of the 2 × 4, to set a reference point. Measure and note the level of the water.

3 Measure the water level every hour on the hour. Note how much the water level drops in each hour. Repeat the test in different areas of the yard and note the results.

HOW TO MAKE A RAIN GAUGE

You can tell how much rain has fallen in your local area with this super simple project.

WHAT YOU'LL NEED

CLEAN, EMPTY TWO-LITER BOTTLE (PREFERABLY CLEAR)

UTILITY KNIFE OR SCISSORS

MARBLES

DUCT TAPE

MASKING TAPE (OPTIONAL)

RULER OR MEASURING TAPE

PERMANENT MARKER

DRAINAGE RATE	SOIL TYPE	RECOMMENDATION
Less than 1 inch (25 mm)/hour	Clay	Improve with compost, stone, and other amendments
1½–2 inches (37.5–50 mm)/hour	Average loamy	Good for most garden plants
3 inches (76 mm)/hour	Light Loam	Fast-draining—best for succulents and drought-tolerant plants
More than 3 inches (76 mm)/hour	Sandy	Improve with soil and moisture-retaining amendments

1 Carefully cut the plastic two-liter bottle along its shoulder (where the bottle neck curves down to the side). Cut all the way around to cut off the top of the bottle. Ask your parents if you can use the utility knife and, if they say "no," use scissors to make this cut.

2 Remove the cap from the top of the bottle and slide the top upside down into the body of the bottle. Tape the top onto the bottom with the cut edges aligned.

Experiments

There are a lot of investigations you can do with your homemade rain gauge.

- Make multiples and measure the rainfall across the yard. Is it the same everywhere?
- Check the gauge regularly, including during the rainy season for the area in which you live. What measurement corresponds to a "heavy" rainfall? Did this surprise you? Why or why not?
- Make a simple rain log and record the weekly totals of rainfall (including dew moisture) in your yard. How could you use this information for planning and planting your garden going forward?

3 Stand the bottle on a flat, level surface and stand the ruler on end next to it. Use the marker to mark 1 inch (2.5 cm) up from bottom, and then every ¼ inch (.6 cm) up to the top. (If your science teacher prefers, you use metric measurements, mark the centimeters.)

4 Drop a few marbles or some gravel into the bottom of the rain gauge, so that it will be stable and won't fall over. Add water up to the 1-inch (2.5 cm) mark.

5 Set the gauge out in a clear area—away from any overhang such as a tree or the roof of a building. You can put the gauge on a table or on an upside-down bucket, but it should sit stable and level. Don't put it on the ground. To record rainfall accurately, your eye should be level with the mark on the bottle.

2 CHOOSE YOUR PLANTS

Now that you understand a bit about how climate and weather will affect your garden, the type of soil you have, and the needs of plants that will grow in the soil, it's time for the most fun part of gardening. You're going to pick your plants!

Standing in front of a rack of seed packets or leafing through a nursery catalog are ways to imagine all your garden could be. There are so many possibilities to choose from! Of course, plants cost money and gardening takes time and effort, so it's only smart to do a little homework and pick the plants that appeal most to you, will thrive in your garden, and won't waste your time or (your parents') money.

A garden is a symphony and that makes you the conductor. This chapter is all about helping you decide what the music in your garden sounds like—whether you're going to grow a more edible garden, something purely for beauty, or a combination. Whether you're planting a whole backyard or just one container, take your time and learn about plants in general, and you'll always have that knowledge to rely on.

QUESTIONS THIS CHAPTER ANSWERS

- What are the best fruits and vegetables to grow in the home garden?
- What makes a fruit, a fruit?
- Why are some plant names so strange?
- What are the growing forms of different garden plants?
- What are the parts of a flower?
- What is the difference between a tree and a shrub?

NATURE'S GROCERY: FRUIT & VEGGIES

Fruits and vegetables are some of the most rewarding plants to grow because you can eat them and they're delicious! Not only that, but if you avoid using chemicals around your plants, you'll be growing edibles that are healthier than what your parents might find in the grocery store. Growing your own also gives you the chance to experiment with varieties and even types of fruit and vegetables that you may not find in any local stores.

FRUIT

Want to grow nature's candy? Then you'll be planting a small annual, a bush, a tree, or a vine. Some fruit can be grown in more than one form. For instance, grape vines are usually grown upright tied to a support, which makes them look more like small trees than vines. But grapes can be left to sprawl or trained along a fence. Bush fruits include those that grow like a shrub (blueberries) and those called "cane berries" (blackberries and raspberries), which sprawl out and have thick stems and small leaves. Although many types of fruit grow on trees, you'll have to wait a long time after planting the tree before you ever see any fruit—sometimes years.

Choose a fruit for your garden based on what you want to eat, how much work you're willing to do, and how long you are willing to wait to enjoy your harvest. Here are nine fantastic and common fruit plants for the beginning gardener to grow.

FRUIT	FORM
Apple	Tree
Apricot	Tree
Blackberry	Caning Fruit
Blueberry	Bush
Cantaloupe	Vine
Cherry	Tree
Currant	Bush
Elderberry	Bush
Figs	Tree
Gooseberry	Bush
Grapes	Vine
Honeydew	Vine
Lemon	Tree
Lime	Tree
Orange	Tree
Peach	Tree
Pear	Tree
Pomegranate	Tree
Pumpkin	Vine
Raspberry	Caning Fruit
Strawberry	Annual Plant
Watermelon	Vine

Blackberries: Talk to your parents before you plant blackberry canes—they are aggressive and can quickly take over a yard. As yummy as the berries are, the canes are thorny and hard to work with (but there are "thornless" varieties). These make good large-container plants. All blackberry plants like a lot of moisture and rich, nutritious soil. These plants are perennial at their roots, but the canes (stems) only last two years. Then they will need to be cut back to allow new-growth canes to flourish and give the best harvest possible. Proper pruning affects how productive blackberry plants are, and it must be done at specific times during the year, so ask for advice from the nursery where you bought the plants.

Blueberries: There are four types of garden blueberry plants: highbush, lowbush, hybrid half-high, and rabbiteye. The most common type sold online or at nurseries is a highbush. Plant new blueberry bushes in early spring, in a bright, sunny location shielded from strong wind. These attractive bushes like acidic soil, between 4 to 5 pH. Blueberries are good container plants and will give you a nice crop during the same period every year.

A blueberry bush in a pot is a great addition to a container kitchen garden.

Cantaloupe & Honeydew Melons: Homegrown cantaloupe are noticeably sweeter and more flavorful than what you'll find at a store. Honeydew melons are grown in a similar way and can be just as delicious, but they are less sweet. Both are "sprawlers," growing on long vines full of large leaves; the plants take up a lot of room (you can grow them up tall, wide trellises but you'll need to support the heavy fruit). They also need two to three months of serious summer heat. If the summers where you live are short or mild, these may not be the plants for your garden. The best cantaloupe and honeydew come from extremely nutritious soil, and these plants love water. The soil should be kept moist.

This deep purple colors signals that this fig is ready to be picked and enjoyed.

Figs: Although fig trees grow best in warmer climates such as zone 8 or above, many gardeners grow this delicious, sticky sweet fruit in containers that are insulated against the cold. There are many different types and varieties— buy one meant for the home gardener in your area; (some

What's in a Name?

Plant names can be a little confusing because most plants have more than one name. There is their "common" name (for instance, "strawberry"), and then they have a scientific Latin name (strawberry's is *Fragaria*). The Latin name is longer if the plant is a mix between two other plants, called a hybrid (the most common strawberry is *Fragaria × ananassa*). Whoever develops a particular variety of the plant will add a unique name for that variety (like *Fragaria × ananassa* 'Alaska Pioneer', which was bred to grow in colder-than-normal temperatures). Knowing the different parts of plant names helps you read seed packets and catalogs, but it's more important to know specifics like sun exposure, how often that plant produces fruit, and other information. You'll find all that on the seed packet or by asking the professionals selling seedlings or plants.

are hard to cultivate and won't tolerate even mild cold). If your fig tree lives in a container, you will need to feed it nitrogen over the course of a season (use an organic fertilizer). You can bring a fig tree into a garage or shed over the winter to make sure it doesn't die of cold. Otherwise, the plant isn't fussy and will provide you with a nice crop of juicy figs every year (pick some of the small, unripe fruit early on and the remaining figs will grow larger).

Grapes: Grapes are fun to grow and long lasting—the same vine can produce fruit for thirty years! Buy "American" grapes, which are better for eating;

"European" and "European-American" grapes are best for winemaking. It's smartest to plant what are known as bare-root plants (there is no dirt around the roots when you buy them). Grapes are usually grown up a support, which can be a structure such as a pergola, a trellis, or even a fence. The most important part of growing grapes is proper pruning. Before the first winter after you plant, cut the top off the cane so that side branches grow out from the main cane. Every season, cut off canes that grew fruit, and prune back new canes so that they only have five buds on them. Prune out measly, weak canes.

Pumpkins: Pumpkins are just plain fun, but you have to be patient; they take a long time to grow. They also take up a lot of room, like other vine-growing fruits and vegetables. Pumpkin plants grow from seed planted in the ground—but the soil has to be warm, at least 70°F (21°C). Enrich the soil with plenty of composted manure and plant the seeds in tall, mounded rows called "hills." Pumpkin plants also need lots of water. Once the vines start growing, avoid stepping on them because they are easy to damage. Turn pumpkins regularly so they don't develop flat or discolored areas. Put cardboard under a nearly ripe pumpkin to make sure it doesn't decay where it's resting. Cut ripe pumpkins off the vine with sharp pruning shears or a knife, leaving a couple inches of stem on the fruit.

Raspberries: The two types of raspberries are summer-fruiting and everbearing. The first provides one crop in summer; the second can produce both a fall and a summer crop. Many gardeners plant both for a season-long supply of berries. Raspberry bushes have to be pruned every year. Canes will only grow fruit for two years, after which they need to be cut out. The plants grow in partial shade or full sun, in well-draining soil protected from wind. You can buy bare-root or potted plants, but either needs to be planted with their crowns 1 to 2 inches (2.5 to 5 cm) above soil level. Although the canes can be left to sprawl, growing on a trellis or fence makes it easier to gather berries and tend the plants.

This everbearing raspberry bush will supply a wealth of berries to the gardener.

Watermelons: Who doesn't love watermelon? It's the perfect summer treat. Even though watermelon grows best in hot climates, "short-season" varieties mature quicker and are good for northern zones (3 to 5). The plants need very rich soil and lots of space. Like pumpkins, they are grown in raised rows, called hills. The plants need a continuous supply of abundant water; mulch around the plants to retain moisture in the soil. Put cardboard under growing fruits to ensure they don't rot where they contact the ground. A watermelon is ripe when you knock on the fruit and it sounds hollow.

Strawberries: These are one of the most popular fruits to grow because they are easy and incredibly delicious. There are three types for the garden—June-bearing, everbearing, and day neutral. June-bearing produce fruit in one blast, over a 2- to 3-week period. Everbearing deliver a big crop of strawberries in spring and fall, and smaller amounts over summer, while day-neutral offer less fruit steadily throughout the season. Nurseries offer bare-root plants and more mature potted plants; most gardeners plant bare-root starts. Strawberries love sun—up to 10 hours a day—and can be grown in the ground or in containers. No matter where they grow, the plants send out "runners" that can create new plants. Strawberries are susceptible both to disease and pests such as slugs, so you should take steps to protect your plants (see page 61 for ways to fight snails and slugs). The trickiest part about strawberries is how you plant them—something many gardeners do incorrectly. Bare-root plants should be planted in wide, shallow holes that don't crimp the roots. All strawberry plants should be planted with the "crown" (the part right above where the roots join into the stem) at soil level. The plants need good air circulation.

THE CURIOUS CASE OF NUTS

What is a nut? It doesn't seem to fit into any category but its own. Actually a nut is a hard, dry fruit. The shell is a seed coat, and the nut meat itself is a seed! This book doesn't cover growing nuts because nuts grow on trees and can be finicky and take years of cultivation, as well as a lot of work to prepare them for eating.

These clusters of cashews needed a tropical climate to grow—not something most backyard gardeners have.

What Makes a Fruit, a Fruit?

You might think you know exactly what a fruit is, but do you? It's a question that botanists have debated for a long time. The botanical definition of a fruit is basically "any seed-bearing edible that grows from the ovary of a flowering plant." All other edibles—those that grow from roots, leaves, flowers, or stems—are considered "vegetables." Too bad it's not quite that simple.

Think an apple is a fruit? That's understandable. After all, the apple tree grows flowers, which are cross-pollinated by bees (thanks, bees!). They fertilize the ovary in the base of the flower, and the ovary develops into an apple, which contains seeds. So you'd be right—the apple checks all the boxes. It is a fruit.

But what about tasty tomatoes? Mom and Dad probably think a tomato is a vegetable. That's usually how growers, sellers, and the law regard them. Consider this, though: a yellow blossom grows on the tomato plant. It is fertilized by pollinators, and the ovary at the base of the flower grows into a tiny green tomato. That eventually grows into a mature tomato. Sounds a lot like how the apple grows, right? Bingo. You have a fruit.

That's why you'll hear teachers and other professionals talk about "botanical classification" versus "culinary classification." That means the science of plants says one thing, but the practice of cooking says another. It's two ways of grouping fruits and vegetables, with some crossover. Generally speaking, culinary classifications consider any edible that is purely sweet, or a combination or tart and sweet (looking at you, lemon), as a fruit. All other edibles with more complex flavor profiles—like a tomato that is sweet, acidic, and uniquely flavored variety to variety—are lumped into the "vegetable" category.

VALUABLE VEGETABLES

If you don't like vegetables, it's probably because you've never tasted one fresh from your own garden. Here are ten awesome options for beginning gardeners.

Beans: Green beans are supereasy to grow and don't take much room. Grow "bush" beans in a container or "pole" beans up a trellis or support. Bush beans are easier, and the beans are ready all at once; pole beans offer a bigger harvest over a longer period. Either is easily grown from seeds. Beans need a regular and heavy supply of water and you should weed around your plants regularly. Pick beans when young and tender, by snapping or cutting them off the plant—usually when the beans are about as thick as a pencil.

Bell Peppers: Eaten fresh or cooked, bell peppers are a favorite because they tasty, easy, and even fun to grow. They need fast-draining soil and have a long growing season. Most gardeners start pepper plants from seedlings, which grow into lovely small bush forms. The plants like slightly acidic soil and are heat-sensitive. Water every day in the heat of summer. Although you may think green and

As bell peppers mature, they change from green to whatever color the variety is meant to be (red, yellow, or orange), sweetening in the process.

red or yellow peppers are from different plants, they're just harvested at different times. Pick a green pepper when it is at its largest, or let it mature and it will turn whatever color the variety is meant to be (it will also get sweeter in the process).

Carrots: There are all kinds of interesting carrots to grow, from rainbow colored ones to ball-shaped varieties. Every one of them likes fast-draining, slightly sandy soil. Grow your carrots from seed, not transplants. Water often, but just a little bit at a time—just enough to make it down to the growing carrot. Eventually, tiny leaves will show on top of the soil, which is a sign that your carrots are headed toward maturity. Don't be afraid to pull up your carrots a little early; younger carrots will have all the flavor—and sometimes more—and be more tender than those that are allowed to grow to full size.

Corn: Although you won't get much of a harvest from a single plant, sweet corn is still one of the tastiest, most enjoyable plants to grow in the backyard garden. For proper pollination, the plants should be grown in groups rather than in straight lines. Corn prefers nearly perfect soil, one that drains well but holds moisture and has tons of nutrients. Add a lot of compost, aged manure, and other amendments. Plant seeds rather than transplants and, if you live in

a colder area, warm the soil for a week first with a layer of black plastic. Plant the seeds about 4 inches (10 cm) apart. Once the plants have grown a little bit, thin them out so that those left are about a foot apart. You'll know the corn is ready to be picked once the silk "tassel" at the top of the ear turns brown and each ear gets noticeably fatter. Pull the ear down while twisting it in order to harvest. Eat the same day for the best flavor.

Cucumbers: There are two types of cucumber plants that grow just like they sound: bush and vining. Bush varieties are better for growing in containers or where space is limited; vining types will produce more cucumbers and can—and should—be grown up a trellis. These plants are cold-sensitive, so you should only plant them outside well after the last frost date. A very sunny location is best. More than anything, though, cucumbers need a steady and abundant supply of water. Pick them as soon as they reach the mature size listed on the seed packet or recommended by the nursery; if you let them grow too big or if they start to turn yellow, they will be bitter. Once the crop comes in, continue harvesting cucumbers every couple of days.

Leaf Lettuces: This is another gardener favorite that puts store-bought versions to shame. Even if you don't usually like salad, you're sure to enjoy the rich flavors of fresh-cut leaf lettuces. There are many types to choose from and most gardeners grow a mixture. Leaf lettuces are those meant to be harvested leaf by leaf, as opposed to head lettuces such as romaine, which are harvested by the whole head at once. Unlike other garden vegetables, leaf lettuces prefer the cooler temperatures of spring and fall—they will "bolt" in hot summer, meaning they will go to seed and produce only bitter leaves. The plants need very rich soil to grow their best, and you should sprinkle them with water whenever the leaves appear a little wilted. Plant in spring and you can plant another crop in late summer or fall. Pick or cut the leaves from the outside of the plant in the morning; younger and smaller leaves will be more tender and flavorful. Large, mature leaves can be bitter.

When these snap peas are picked, they will be so fresh that they will snap when broken open—which is where their name comes from.

Peas: Both nutritious and tasty raw or cooked, peas are a great choice for a summer garden. Choose from three basic types of peas: English peas, snow peas, or snap peas. English peas have to be shelled (taken out of their pods) to be eaten. The other two can be eaten whole. Snap peas are the most popular for home gardeners. Regardless of the variety, their growing season isn't long. These are cool-weather plants that are planted early in spring, even while there is still danger of frost. Plant in spring and fall for two crops. Peas like full sun, well-draining soil, and don't need the soil to be amended (adding nutrients can cause more leaves and fewer peas). Grow peas on a support such as poles, a trellis, or a fence. Water plants moderately and consistently but be careful when weeding because it's easy to damage their shallow roots. Start picking two months after planting; harvest in the morning, holding the stem with one hand and removing the pod with the other.

Radishes: Radishes are yet another cool-weather crop, and many gardeners will plant seeds every 10 days to get a big crop of radishes. The seeds are planted a couple weeks before the last frost, and then again in the fall. The plants should be thinned to 2 inches (5 cm) apart. Water consistently and evenly. This vegetable only takes about 3 weeks to be ready for harvest, and you should pull up one to see if the crop is ready (don't leave them in the ground past maturity or they'll quickly become inedible).

Tomatoes: These are the jewel of the summer garden. Try different varieties each year because they all have their own charms. Experiment with different sizes and shapes, including plum, Roma, beefsteak, and cherry. Some are grown for slicing, while others, such as grape tomatoes, can be popped right in your mouth for a juicy treat any-time. The two basic types of tomato plant are *determinate* (they grow to a set size) and *indeterminate* (they'll keep on growing as long as conditions are right). Tomatoes can be a little challenging to grow because pests and even wildlife like them as much as humans do, and they are susceptible to disease. They grow best in slightly acidic soil but can thrive in most soils if their needs are met. The plants should receive six hours of strong direct sun a day and should be watered deeply to encourage strong root growth. You can grow your tomatoes in the ground but cultivating them in containers gives you a lot more control. Drip irrigation or heavy mulch will prevent water from splashing on the leaves, something that could lead to disease. Water in the early morning. Grow them in tomato cages, available at nurseries and home-improvement centers (the cages support the plants, especially as the branches become heavy with fruit). Pick tomatoes when they reach their mature size, are firm, and are evenly colored. Carefully twist them off the stem to avoid hurting the plant.

Zucchini: Zucchini is a type of squash and most squashes are grown in the same way—on long, thick vines. You can make growing them easier (and limit the space they'll take up) by training the vines up a trellis or on some other support. Zucchini plants need rich, well-draining soil and full sun. They can't tolerate cold; plant transplants after the weather has begun to warm. Plant fewer than ten plants—they will produce more zucchini than you can use. The plants set their fruit from the beautiful yellow blossoms, but you can pinch off some of the blossoms to eat—they are incredible when deep fried. Harvest individual zucchini before the skin gets hard, when the fruit is about 6 inches (15 cm) long. Cut zucchini at the stem with a sharp knife being careful not to damage the plant or your hands.

Perfect Partners

Did you know that veggies naturally have BFFs? It's true. Some plants grow better together. This is called *companion planting*. In some cases, the natural defenses of one plant will protect the other against natural pests. Or one plant will draw totally different nutrients from the soil, leaving plenty of good stuff for its partner. Certain flowers might attract pollinators that a fruit plant needs to bear fruit. Here are some common plant combinations you might consider when choosing what to grow in your garden.

Bell Peppers & Basil: Common bell pepper pests hate basil, so the herb helps keep the veggies safe from attack.

Cucumbers & Nasturtiums: Beetles that eat cucumbers don't like nasturtiums. They'll go elsewhere for a meal.

Carrots & Tomatoes: Tomatoes provide shade and produce a natural insecticide against carrot pests.

Corn & Green Beans: Beans fix nitrogen in the soil, which helps corn thrive; corn stalks provide a trellis for the beans to climb.

Marigolds & Tomatoes: The pretty marigolds help protect tomato plants against root nematodes that can cause a lot of damage.

Borage & Cabbages: Borage grows pretty, edible blue flowers and repels cabbage worms and tomato hornworms—which means it's also a good partner for tomatoes and even strawberries.

HERBS FOR FUN

Herbs are tasty, easy, and fun to grow. They add flavor to a lot of different foods. Don't plant herbs in any area of the yard or garden that has been treated with pesticides or other chemicals (ask Mom and Dad to be sure), because the herbs will pick up the chemicals and you could wind up consuming them.

Basil: A great container plant, basil is grown as an annual. Choose from several types; the most common is sweet basil. Lemon basil tastes like its name sounds. Purple basil really is purple, and Thai basil tastes a little like licorice! All are easy to grow. Plant transplants as soon as the soil warms. Basil likes heat, but don't expose it to cold nights.

Water basil consistently in soil that drains well. As soon as the plant grows about six leaves, pinch it back to the first set of leaves and it will grow really bushy and full. When the plant is 8 inches (20 cm) tall, start picking the bigger leaves to use on salads, or eat them with tomatoes and cheese. Pick bigger leaves even if you won't use them, because it will help the plant keep producing. Pick all the leaves at the end of the season, right before the weather gets cold.

Dill fronds are a unique and pretty visual in the garden, and the light licorice aroma is wonderful as well.

Thyme is a handsome garden plant that produces plenty of leaves for cooking and small, clustered flowers in spring.

Dill: Dill is an annual with a light licorice flavor and is a good garden addition for its aroma and weird fronds. This herb grows best when planted in the ground as seed, as soon as any threat of frost has passed. If you're growing cabbage, grow the dill right next to it, but don't plant dill close to carrots. Cut off fronds when the plant has five or six leaves or fronds. Many gardeners plant dill seeds every couple of weeks to have the herb all summer.

Rosemary: Rosemary is an evergreen. Its needles taste great in a lot of different dishes, and a single healthy plant can supply most of the rosemary you'll ever need. Plant transplants in a container or the ground after the last frost in your area. Make sure the soil drains well—rosemary is tolerant of dry, hot conditions but won't do well if it gets too much water. Snip off up to a third of the new growth at any one time and it will grow back.

Sage: Gardeners grow sage for its wonderful aroma, savory flavor, and because it is easy to grow! Fuzzy silvery green leaves and purple flower stalks in spring make this a nice addition to a garden. Plant transplants or seeds when any possibility of frost has passed. Sage likes a hot, dry location and doesn't like to stand in wet soil (it also doesn't do well near cucumbers). Once the plant is established, after about a month, cut off the small sprigs and leaves on the outside of the plant. Harvest the plant a couple of times in the first year, and possibly three the next. Don't cut sprigs when it's close to winter because the plant needs to store energy. Sage is a perennial.

Thyme: Thyme grows like a low shrub and is a perennial. Grow your thyme from transplants, which is much easier than starting from seed. The most common type is English thyme, but you can also plant lemon thyme, which smells slightly of lemon, or caraway thyme, which tastes a little bit like caraway seeds. This herb loves the heat and will do best in strong direct sun and soil that doesn't hold moisture. (It will grow well near rosemary because the two like similar conditions.) Harvest thyme in just a couple of "crops" each season by clipping off the new, tender growth on the outside of the plant.

FASCINATING FLOWERS

Flowers are fun, beautiful, and easy to grow. They are like decorations for your garden. More importantly, they attract important insects to the garden. Most garden flowers are annuals, but there are many flowering perennials as well. Gardeners plant annuals to have a different look every year. Perennials, however, are good choices where you want a low-maintenance plant that is best for a certain location, like along a walkway.

10 FAVORITE ANNUAL FLOWERS

These are the most popular flowering annuals gardeners grow. Because they are annuals, you can plant them no matter what zone you live in. Keep in mind that you'll find many other flowering plants and varieties at your local nursery or home center—explore to discover the ones that are just right for your garden.

Cornflower (*Centaurea cyanus*): These frilly, beautiful, bright blue flowers (some varieties are white or even shades of red) are eye-catching anywhere in the garden. They are great cut flowers.

STARTING: Plant seeds or transplants in early spring; cornflower can tolerate early-season cold. Mulch around seedlings to prevent weeds. Plants should be kept about 12 inches (30 cm) apart, which may mean thinning those planted from seeds.

CARE: Weed regularly and keep the soil a little moist but don't soak it. Cornflower is drought-tolerant, so it's better in dry soil than overly wet soil. If you've picked a tall-growing variety, stake the flower stems as they mature. These are good for cutting and for drying. The flowers are also edible!

Geranium (*Pelagornium*): Geraniums are grown like an annual in most gardens but they are a perennial in the warmest zones. These are a container gardening favorite because of their nice fragrance and beautiful flowers and foliage; you'll find varieties that are fire-engine red to blue to pink, with mottled, hairy leaves.

STARTING: You can plant them from seedlings, but if you want your own geraniums year after year, take cuttings from plants at the end of the season and grow the cuttings indoors. Cultivate them in a pot in a sunny location.

CARE: Geraniums like their soil to dry out between waterings, and they should be regularly deadheaded.

Cornflowers' unique blooms will stand out in any flower garden.

Impatiens are a low-maintenance, long-blooming favorite of flower gardeners.

Their distinctive ink-blot faces give pansies a lot of character and draw attention to their brightly colored flowers. The flowers are edible.

Impatiens: Also known as "Busy Lizzie," this low-growing annual is used in containers and the front of flower beds, where it offers splashes of red, purple, pink, and white.

    STARTING: Impatiens should be transplanted after all danger of frost has passed. They will do well in most soils.

    CARE: Impatiens tolerate shade, but they need consistent watering.

Marigold (*Tagetes*): Marigolds come in different shades of gold, yellow, and white and are some of the easiest flowers you can plant.

    STARTING: You can plant marigolds from seed, but most gardeners use transplants. Plant in the ground or in containers in late spring in full sun.

    CARE: Pinch the tops off young plants to encourage bushy growth. Water regularly at the base of the plants, not on their leaves.

Petunia: These easy-to-grow plants are annuals everywhere except zones 9 to 11. They are a gardener favorite because they thrive with little tending, will grow in full shade, and come in just about every color of the rainbow.

    STARTING: Although you can grow them from seeds, most gardeners opt for the easier option of transplants. Petunias like nutritious, well-drained soil, and they should be sheltered from wind.

    CARE: Petunias are somewhat drought-tolerant and will forgive you if you forget to water them for a couple of days.

Nasturtium (*Tropaeolum*): These are ideal flowers for the beginning gardener because they are not fussy, they grow quickly, and they smell nice.

    STARTING: Nasturtiums are easy to grow from seed or transplants, and they do equally well in containers and in the ground.

    CARE: These plants are fine with less nutritious soils and will tolerate some shade. Water the plants regularly but be careful not to overwater. The flowers are edible!

Pansy (*Viola × wittrockiana*): These are pure fun flowers with "faces" of black blotches on the bright yellow or purple flowers. They are great for containers of any kind, and they will grow in garden beds as well. Although technically a perennial in certain parts of the country, the vast majority of gardeners grow pansies as annuals.

STARTING: Pansies like the cool and can even survive a frost. Plant them in spring or fall, or both—they won't survive over a hot summer. You can start seeds indoors, but most people buy transplants at the very start of the gardening season. Although they thrive in full sun, pansies are okay with partial shade. Keep in mind that the plants will spread 10 to 12 inches (25.5 to 30 cm).

CARE: Pansies need regular watering and should be deadheaded to encourage more flowers.

Snapdragon (*Antirrhinum majus*): These unusual garden bed standouts grow clusters of flowers on tall stems. Different varieties feature blooms in all the colors of a painter's palette, and you can pick from dwarf, medium, and tall varieties.

STARTING: The seeds and seedlings like cool soil; these should be some of the first flowers you plant in the garden in late winter or early spring, just as the weather starts to warm. Most gardeners prefer transplants, but you can start seeds indoors a few weeks before the last frost date. In either case, harden off seedlings before planting. Plant snapdragons in rich soil in full sun.

The spiky flower clusters make the shape of snapdragons an interesting addition to a cut-flower garden.

CARE: Once plants are established, clip their tops to encourage bushy growth and more flowers. Water regularly at the base of the plant and stake taller varieties as they mature.

Sunflower (*Helianthus*): These are fantastic summer cut-flower garden additions (in the back row). The large brown centers of these yellow flowers hold a bunch of edible seeds!

STARTING: Sunflowers are easy to grow from seeds as long as you plant them after the danger of any frost. Give them lots of space—plants should be 30 inches (75 cm) apart.

CARE: Water sunflower plants deeply, but not often (to encourage deep root growth). As the plants grow tall, you may need to tie them to a support so that they don't bend under their own weight. Cut the flowers in the morning. Cut an unopened flower bud off a stem and other blooms will grow off that stem.

Zinnia: These are ideal flowers for a cut-flower garden because the plant produces so many blooms over the season. Their pom-pom blooms grow on long stems in a multitude of dusty colors.

STARTING: Grow zinnias in containers or in garden beds (you can choose from shorter or taller varieties). The plants are sensitive to cold, so most gardeners plant transplants long after any chance of frost has passed. The plants love strong direct sun and rich, quick-draining soil. Give them plenty of room so that they can spread out and bloom as much as possible (up to 20 inches (51 cm) apart). They need good air circulation to avoid diseases.

CARE: Deadhead regularly to encourage new blooms. Water moderately; zinnias aren't thirsty plants.

6 FAVORITE PERENNIALS

Choosing a flowering perennial is a bigger decision for a gardener because you'll live with your choice for quite a while. Pick perennials that really appeal to you.

Coneflower (*Echinacea*): These are wonderful, pretty flowering plants that attract birds and butterflies to your garden. The flowers are shaped like daisies, but with a big round knob in the middle. Although purple is the most well-known and popular coneflower color, there are many other colors available.

    STARTING: These plants grow big, so leave at least 1 foot (30 cm) and up to 3 feet (91 cm) between plants. They'll fill in the difference! Start seeds indoors a couple of weeks before the last frost date or do what most gardeners do—grow from potted transplants that you put in the soil in mid-spring just as the weather and soil warm. (If you start yours from seed, they may take up to three years before their first blooms.)

    CARE: Coneflowers are drought-tolerant and can do well in poor soil, but they prefer a nutritious base; regularly add a thick layer of compost around the plants, which will feed them and protect against weeds.

Coneflowers are attention-getters in any garden but need lots of room to grow.

Coreopsis: The most common varieties of coreopsis produce stunning flowers with bright yellow petals splashed with dark red centers. They are wonderful in a cut-flower garden or any large flower bed.

    STARTING: Most beginning gardeners transplant potted coreopsis plants from a nursery. Grow yours from seed if you prefer, starting three weeks before the final frost date. Plant coreopsis at the end of spring or in early summer, when soil temperatures are consistently 70°F (21°C) or above. (Harden off seedlings before planting.) Coreopsis like rich, well-draining soil in a site that receives abundant direct sun.

    CARE: Mulch heavily around the plants and weed regularly. Water in the mornings and keep the soil moist to a depth of 1 inch (2.5 cm).

Daylily (*Hemerocallis*): They are called "daylily" because the blooms only last a day. But there are often a dozen to a stem, so you'll have flowers for weeks. And, oh, what flowers! There is an astounding number of colors and forms available. The flowers grow over pretty, green, swordlike foliage.

    STARTING: Start with plants bought at a nursery, home improvement center, or by mail order. You won't need to put a lot of effort into improving the soil unless it doesn't drain well—daylilies like moist but not soaking wet soil. Plant them in mid-spring while the weather is still cool.

    CARE: Daylilies don't need much tending (they are low maintenance). They should be divided (see page 57) after a few years, when they start producing fewer flowers. Otherwise, water them regularly and enjoy the flowers.

Lavender (*Lavandula*): Lavender's tiny purple or blue flowers are clustered on long stems, and they add an unforgettably nice aroma to the garden. This bushy plant loves hot sun and can do well even in drought conditions and in poor soil.

    STARTING: The best time to plant your lavender is in mid- to late spring, just as the soil begins to warm. Most gardeners buy potted plants and transplant them; leave 2 to 3 feet (.6 to .9 meters) between plants because lavender grows bushy and full.

Peonies are showy flowers that grow bushy and can fill out a whole bed by themselves.

CARE: You only need to water lavender twice a week to keep it happy. Cut the flower stems after at least half the buds on the plant have opened. Harvest the flowers in the morning and cut the stem as far down as possible. They are wonderful in arrangements, but also make great dried flowers that can be used to scent fabrics and flavor food.

Peony: Peonies are some of the most beautiful garden flowers, with varieties that bloom pink, red, or white (and some in patterns of two colors).

STARTING: Transplant bare-root peonies in the middle of fall before the cold weather really sets in. These plants need a location with full sun exposure and nutritious soil that drains well. Dig a large hole 24 inches (60 cm) across and 24 inches (60 cm) deep and amend as necessary. Mound dirt so that the tuber is only about 2 inches (5 cm) below soil level and then fill in the hole. Leave about 4 feet (1.2 meters) between a peony and other plants. Water thoroughly right after planting.

CARE: Don't worry if you see ants all over the flowerbuds in spring. They eat peony nectar and keep the plant safe from other bugs. Stake oversized flowers if the weight is causing the stems to bend over. Deadhead the flowers regularly as they fade (or cut young flowers in the morning, to put in a vase).

The rich blue-purple salvia flowers look especially cool when paired with orange flowers such as sunflowers or marigolds.

Salvia (*Salvia officinalis*): These are bushy plants with beautiful spiky often purple flowers. They are great to fill in a bed. Some salvias, such as pineapple sage, are annuals.

STARTING: Plant potted plants right after the last frost in your area. Leave between 2 and 3 feet (.6 to .9 meters) between plants. Amend the soil first, to make sure it's very nutritious and drains well.

CARE: Mulch to keep down weeds and keep the soil moist throughout the growing season. Cut off fading blooms to encourage flowering.

Black-eyed Susan (*Rudbeckia hirta*): These are distinctive wildflowers grown as perennials in many areas, and as annuals in cooler parts of the country. Gold or yellow blooms with big, dark brown centers make these perfect for the cut-flower garden.

STARTING: Plant from seed or transplants in late spring after the soil has warmed. They like lots of sun, consistent water (ideally the soil should always be a little moist), and nutritious, quick-draining soil. Give each plant plenty of room—about 18 inches (46 cm) apart—to grow and produce lots of blooms.

CARE: Deadhead the flowers to promote more blooms.

EDIBLE FLOWERS

Did you know that fruits and vegetables aren't the only edibles in your garden? Some flowers can be eaten and look beautiful on a plate or in a salad. *But be very careful: Never eat any plant out of your garden unless you are absolutely sure that it is safe for human consumption. If you have any doubts, ask an adult.*

Borage is grown for its beauty, medicinal, and edible uses, and for the borage blossoms with their delicate, pretty blue flowers. They are often used to accent salads or are used as garnish on dinner plates.

Lavender flowers can be crushed to flavor sweets from cupcakes to ice cream, and the flowers can be used as a pretty accent on cakes and salads. Be careful, though, the flowers can be a strong flavoring.

Nasturtiums have a subtle, peppery flavor. They are excellent pretty additions to a tossed green salad.

Pansies don't really have much taste at all, but the flowers are incredibly pretty. Bakers coat them with crushed sugar, and then use them as decorations on cakes and other baked goods.

Sage blossoms can be dipped in batter and fried; they taste a little like chicken nuggets.

Tulips taste a little like an apple; don't eat the structure inside, but you can clean out the flower and eat the leaves. Fill a hollowed-out tulip bloom with tuna salad!

TREES & SHRUBS

Trees and shrubs are some of the most expensive garden plants because they don't grow as quickly as vegetables and flowers do. It's handy to know a little bit about them if and when you want to add any to your garden.

Gardeners often plant trees or shrubs as *specimens* or *groupings*. A specimen plant is planted for its distinctive appearance. It is given space all to itself or a garden bed is designed around it to showcase the tree or shrub. Groupings are just like they sound—several trees and shrubs are planted for a purpose, such as creating a living fence, providing a privacy screen, or hiding an unattractive feature.

Shrubs and trees can be *deciduous* (their leaves fall off in response to either cold or dry weather) or *evergreen* (they grow needles that only fall off as they are replaced by new ones).

SHRUBS

A shrub is taller and fuller than a bush (although there isn't much scientific difference between the two), but it is shorter and has more stems than a tree. Some plants can be grown in either shrub or tree form.

The 5 Best Foliage Shrubs

Arborvitae (*Thuja*): This quick-growing, sturdy evergreen is often planted in rows, close together to create an always-green privacy hedge or living fence.

    ZONES: 2 to 7

    SIZE: 3 feet (.9 meter) wide × 3 to 20 feet (.9 to 6 meters) tall

    CONDITIONS: Full sun for at least 6 hours a day; water weekly if it hasn't rained.

Boxwood (*Buxus*): A classic border shrub that is often pruned into formal or decorative shapes from balls to animal sculptures. Sturdy and low growing, boxwoods are low maintenance.

    ZONES: 5 to 9

    SIZE: 2 to 4 feet (.6 to 1.2 meters) wide × 3 to 9 feet (.9 to 2.7 meters) tall

    CONDITIONS: Morning sun with afternoon shade; water three times a week, keeping soil moist to 1 inch (2.5 cm) deep, but not soggy.

GARDEN JARGON

The word *topiary* describes the technique of pruning or clipping shrubs and trees into ornamental shapes—such as animals or swirling cones. It is a little bit art and a little bit science; the gardener has to envision the shape and then know how to clip it without damaging the plant. You can try pruning a topiary starting with simple shapes such as a pyramid or globe.

CHOOSE YOUR PLANTS

The gold dust plant's leaves are endlessly fascinating.

Gold Dust Plant (*Aucuba japonica* 'Variegata'): A unique foliage plant, the gold dust plant's leaves look just like the name describes: like someone sprinkled gold flakes on its light green leaves. They plant is more fascinating the closer you get to it, and it's an excellent choice for a container shrub. This rugged specimen will tolerate occasional extremely cold weather and even poor soil.

    ZONES: 6 to 10

    SIZE: Maximum 6 feet (1.8 meters) wide × 10 feet (3 meters) tall

    CONDITIONS: Partial shade; water once a week although the plant is drought tolerant.

Golden Euonymus (*Euonymus japonicus*): This particular member of the Euonymus family has intriguing, light green leaves covered with splotches of bright yellow. It's low maintenance, although it does require fertile, well-draining soil.

    ZONES: 6 to 9

    SIZE: Maximum 6 feet (1.8 meters) wide × 10 feet (3 meters) tall

    CONDITIONS: Partial to full sun; water weekly, fertilize at the start of the season.

Holly (*Ilex*): Although the dark green, pointy (ouch!) leaves are attractive, most people grow holly for its bright red berries. There are many varieties of holly. All grow best in well-draining, slightly acidic soil.

    ZONES: 5 to 9

    SIZE: Some holly varieties can grow up to 10 feet (3 meters) wide × 30 feet (9 meters) tall.

    CONDITIONS: Partial shade; water 2 inches (5 cm) per week for mature plants.

5 Best Flowering Shrubs

Azalea: Blazing with pink, purple, yellow, white, orange, or red blossoms, this flowering shrub is a favorite of gardeners everywhere. It's easy to grow but does require slightly acidic soil.

    ZONES: 6 to 9

    SIZE: Up to 5 feet (1.5 meters) wide × 6 feet (1.8 meters) tall

    CONDITIONS: Morning sun, afternoon shade; water deeply once a week.

Butterfly Bush (*Buddleia davidii*): Super easy to grow, butterfly bush is a favorite for its conical flowerheads that bloom in fun shades of pink, white, and purple. The shrub attracts lots of butterflies too.

    ZONES: 5 to 10

    SIZE: 5 to 10 feet (1.5 to 3 meters) wide × 6 to 12 feet (1.8 to 3.6 meters) tall

    CONDITIONS: Full sun; water once a week in the absence of rain.

Hydrangea: This is a classic gardener's shrub with large and fluffy white, blue, lavender, pink, or red flowers and a full form that fills in blank spaces in the garden.

    ZONES: 3 to 9

    SIZE: 3 to 12 feet (.9 to 3.6 meters) wide × 3 to 20 feet (.9 to 6 meters) tall

    CONDITIONS: Full sun to partial shade; water regularly and keep soil moist.

Rhododendron: The rhododendron is in the same genus as azaleas. It is, however, a larger plant with large, floppy pink, purple, maroon, or white blooms.

    ZONES: 5 to 8

    SIZE: 2 to 10 feet (.6 to 3 meters) wide × 3 to 20 feet (.9 to 6 meters) tall

    CONDITIONS: Partial shade; water regularly.

Weigela: Another shrub that is easy to grow and simple to maintain, weigela is the pick of many gardeners because of its pretty dark red, pink, or white blossoms in spring and early summer.

> **ZONES:** 5 to 8
> **SIZE:** 2 to 10 feet (.6 to 3 meters) tall and wide
> **CONDITIONS:** Full sun; water once a week in the absence of rain.

TREES

The visible part of any tree is only half the story. On many trees, the root system goes down as deep and spreads as wide as the parts of the tree aboveground. Those roots are very efficient at drawing water and nutrients out of the soil—so efficient, that it can take away what's left for other plants. Trees also shade other plants, which can cool them, but can deprive sun-loving species of much-needed direct sunlight.

Most trees grow slowly and can have long lives. (The oldest tree in the world is considered by scientists to be a bristlecone pine tree in California; they think it is more than 4,500 years old!) That means that planting a tree is a big commitment.

There are smaller trees, such as Japanese maples, that grow very slowly. They are often visually interesting and can be planted as specimen plants or even in a container.

Most gardeners buy trees "balled and burlapped," which are at least a couple years old, larger, with a big round rootball wrapped in burlap (or similar) fabric. Consult the nursery professional if you're ready to add a tree to your garden. You'll want to get it off to a perfect start.

Trees are an environmentally friendly option. Because of their large size and structure, trees store more carbon dioxide (in a process called carbon *sequestration*) than smaller plants such as grasses or flowers. The larger the tree, the more carbon it will store, and evergreens are the best at storing carbon.

Lord of the Rings

You might have heard that you could tell the age of a tree by cutting a slice of the trunk and counting the rings. Well, that's true! Why it's true is a more fascinating fact. Trees grow new layers at the start of spring and summer. The new spring wood is lighter because the cells are bigger; summer growth is slower and denser, making dark rings. That means you can tell the age of the tree simply by counting the dark rings. The rings, however, tell you much more than the passing of time.

Traumatic events such as a fire or a drought will affect tree ring formation. A fire, for instance, will often leave a scar that is captured in a ring. Scientists study the rings of fallen trees to determine the history of an entire forest. That, in turn, gives them a detailed picture of how the weather in a region has changed over time.

Japanese maples grow very slowly, with lovely leaves and color.

3 GARDENING HOW-TOS

Gardening skills and techniques are easy to learn and build up over time. One of the wonderful things about gardening is that you can "learn on the job" while you grow amazing plants. What's even better is that the skills you'll pick up in this chapter can all be used no matter what type of gardening you're doing!

You should start with basic tools and gear. Any gardening is made a lot easier by using the right tools in the correct way. It's a good idea to ask your parents for help choosing and buying quality gardening tools. Well-made tools will help you garden with less effort and more enjoyment. They will also last a lot longer than bargain basement choices.

When it comes to actual techniques, start from the ground up. Want the healthiest, hardiest plants? Start with getting the soil in shape. The information here isn't super complicated, but it's really important.

Once you've mastered tending the soil, you can move on to getting your plants off the best start possible. There are lots of ways to do that, but only one will be right for you. Still, it only makes sense for you to learn other options for reproducing plants. This chapter wraps up with a section you might not need—dealing with pests and diseases. But if you do encounter those problems, it's good to deal with them sooner rather than later.

To guarantee success when growing plants from seeds, seed companies usually recommend planting more than you need in a location, and then *thinning* the seedlings that grow. Thinning is the process of removing seedlings that are smaller and closer to others, so that the remaining seedlings have less competition for resources such as water and soil nutrients.

QUESTIONS THIS CHAPTER ANSWERS

- How do you work safely in the garden?
- What's the best way to add amendments to your soil?
- What are different methods for starting plants? Which is the best?
- How do you maintain your gardening tools?
- How do you properly compost organic materials?
- What should you add to—and what should you keep out of—the compost pile?
- What are the most common pests and diseases and how do you fight them?

THE GREAT GEAR GUIDE

You don't need a lot of tools and equipment to garden, but the ones that you do need are important. Outfit yourself correctly, and you'll be setting up your gardening for success—for years to come!

WEARABLES

The right clothes make gardening easier and more comfortable. Jeans or shorts are great, especially if you're planting a garden in the ground. A sun-blocking hat wide enough to shield your whole face is also a useful piece of clothing for the gardener. Too much sun can cause what's called "heatstroke," which can make you dizzy, dehydrated, and give you a headache.

Sturdy shoes or boots will be more comfortable than flip-flops, sandals, or shoes with openings or holes in them. But the most important piece of clothing will be a quality pair of gardening gloves. These should be puncture-proof and made of a fabric that "breathes"—letting water and sweat evaporate. The best gardening gloves should have a rubberized finger-grip surface.

Safety gear for gardening—and the projects in this book—include high-quality gloves, knee pads if you'll be doing a lot of weeding or kneeling, safety glasses and hearing protection for woodworking projects, and a brimmed hat to avoid too much sun exposure.

SAFETY FIRST!

Once you get a little gardening experience under your belt, you may want to invest in some gear for very specific purposes. One of the most useful additions to your garden tool box is a Hori Hori knife. This is a tough, all-purpose tool that not only can cut things like twine and plant stems, it is also ideal for digging out plants or quickly weeding the garden bed—removing even stubborn weeds.

THE MUST-HAVE TOOLS

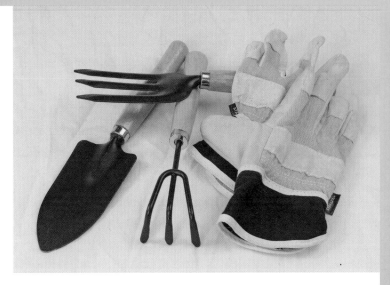

Trowel: It's a simple tool, but a trowel is something you'll use often in your garden. Pick one that is comfortable in your hand and not so large that it's hard to handle or tires your arm out quickly. A padded handle adds comfort but padding materials can trap moisture and dirt. The right shape of a wooden handle will be just as comfortable, especially if you're using gloves. Plastic handles or trowels will break sooner rather than later; invest a little more in a metal trowel.

Garden spade: This tool is like a short, small, square-bladed shovel. It makes digging easier. A stainless steel or carbon blade is best, especially one with rolled or flat "shoe treads" at the top of the blade. The handle should be wood (preferably ash), riveted to the blade. Buy one that works with your height.

Garden fork: A garden fork helps you efficiently and quickly turn soil. The best general-use garden fork has four carbon steel tines and a solid wood handle to which the head and handle are riveted. The handle should be comfortable in your hand, and you should be able to grip it securely and pick up the fork with one hand.

Hoe: Hoes can quickly form rows or plow up weeds. They are pulled or pushed through soil, so they are always working against resistance. That's why your hoe should be well built. Some gardeners use a diamond-head hoe (the blade is pointed), but you'll find a standard square blade hoe is the most useful. Choose a wooden hoe with a rubber grip rather than a fiberglass or plastic handle.

Rake: Gardeners use a garden rake a lot more than a leaf rake. The best garden rake has sturdy steel tines attached to a long metal collar and oversized rivets. Look for a hardwood handle with a grip that's thin enough to wrap your hand around.

Shovel: Although there are many different types of shovels available, the most useful for a gardener is a round-blade shovel with a hardwood or composite handle and a forged or "closed back" blade.

Wheelbarrow: A wheelbarrow can save you a lot of labor. Pick one that is smaller so that you can move it when it is loaded down with supplies, dirt, or rocks. The best have a metal or thick plastic body, two wheels, and pneumatic (air-filled) tires. Rubber hand grips help you keep your grip over rough surfaces.

TOOL CARE

Properly cared for, gardening tools can last decades. Clean tools right after you finish working in the garden. Hose them off or brush off dirt, but don't store them wet. Don't leave tools out in the rain; store them in shed or on a wall under an overhang. Last, use tools only for the purpose they're intended.

TOOLS FOR THE PROJECTS IN THIS BOOK

In addition to basic gardening tools, you'll need some basic woodworking tools to create some of the projects that follow.

Hammer: A basic claw hammer is useful for putting together structures such as raised beds and trellises. Find one that is sized correctly for kid-sized gardeners.

Power drill and bits: A good power drill is super useful for making wooden gardening projects, but you'll have to get permission from your parents—or ask an adult to handle the drilling part of a project—before using a power drill.

SAFETY FIRST

Woodworking power tools are dangerous, which is why you should always ask one of your parents to help you when a project calls for a power tool. Watching your mom or dad safely operate a power saw or sander is a good way to learn, but also ensures that you don't hurt yourself. Some tools, such as a power drill or palm sander, are usually okay for anyone over ten years old to operate, but always check with your parents before ever operating any power tool.

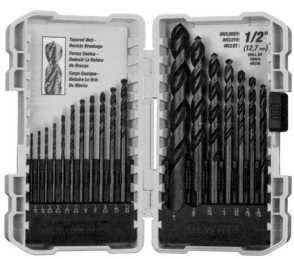

Handsaw: A basic handsaw is the easier and best option for any young gardener who needs to cut a piece of wood to size. Cutting tasks can be done much quicker with a jigsaw, miter saw, circular saw, or table saw. However, those tools can be dangerous and should only ever be operated by an adult.

Sanders: A "palm sander" is the smallest powered sander available and can be used by most kids, as long you have permission from a parent. Larger sanders are more powerful and should only be used by adults. Palm sanders are used with sanding sheets that are cut to fit the pad of the sander, or special sanding sheets sized for the sanders and made with a self-adhesive backing that lets them be affixed to the sanding pad.

HOW TO IMPROVE YOUR SOIL

The soil in your backyard may not be ideal for the plants you choose. Soil can be too acidic or it can drain poorly. That's okay because it's easy to improve the soil and fix those problems. The process is called *amending* the soil. It involves adding ingredients to improve soil in one way or another. You learned a little about soil basics on page 16, but now's the time to really "dig in"!

Amend garden soil in early spring at the beginning of the growing season. But first, test your soil to determine what it needs. Test soil pH (page 20), nutrient levels (page 16), and drainage (see page 23).

ADJUSTING PH

Changing soil acidity is simple. Add sulfur to make it more acidic and add lime to make it more alkaline (less acidic). You simply spread the lime or sulfur evenly over the garden bed, rake it into the soil, and water well. Apply slightly less than the amount recommended on the bag or by a nursery professional. You can always add more later.

FIXING TEXTURE

The best soil allows water to drain steadily and roots to grow unobstructed. Roots that sit in water can rot, but if the soil drains too quickly, the plant won't get enough moisture. Compost is best to improve drainage. It provides a natural, balanced blend of nutrients and creates an ideal texture. Composted manure is also good. (Avoid fresh manure; it may add too much nitrogen, which can "burn" plants.) Peat moss is used to improve soil texture, but it is more expensive than compost and is not an environmentally friendly option. It takes thousands and thousands of years to form, and peat is crucial to wetlands that purify the air and control water movement—harvesting it causes a lot of climate damage.

FIXING NUTRIENTS

You learned in chapter 2 that there are three major chemical nutrients in healthy soil (along with "trace" elements present in much smaller amounts): nitrogen, phosphorus, and potassium. The right amounts of each are essential to plant health. Nitrogen and potassium dissolve in water, so they wash out of soil and are quickly consumed by plants. That's why they regularly need to be replenished. Phosphorus is most important for bulb and root growth, but it also aids flowering. You'll need less of it than the other two.

Correcting a lack of nutrients is usually just a matter of adding fertilizer. There are *organic* and *inorganic* fertilizers available. Organic types are made of natural materials such as bonemeal. Inorganic, or synthetic, fertilizers are made in a lab. Many gardeners and environmentalists use only organic fertilizers because they are less likely to have unexpected results and will work more naturally with plants. Synthetic fertilizers are easier to use and quicker. Regardless of the fertilizer you choose, follow the instructions on the labels to feed plants or improve your soil.

IF YOU HAVE	AMEND WITH
Acidic soil	Lime
Alkaline soil	Sulfur, ammonium sulfate
Poor drainage	Gypsum, compost, peat, perlite
Fast-draining soil	Composted manure, sphagnum peat moss
Low potassium	Wood ash, kelp meal, potassium sulfate
Low nitrogen	Chicken manure, grass cuttings, cottonseed meal
Low phosphorus	Bonemeal, rock phosphate

There are many different soil amendments available, but be careful to choose the right one for your soil and plants.

HOW TO COMPOST

Gardeners call compost "black gold" because it is so rich and useful in the garden. You can make all the compost you need right at home with little effort. And you'll not only improve your soil, you'll help the environment.

Compost is decomposing (rotting) organic matter. You can buy bags of compost, but it's super easy to make. Many materials can be composted, but garden compost is usually made from household and yard waste such as vegetable peels and leaves. All compost piles require heat, oxygen, and water to break down whatever is being composted. You can compost in a pile in the corner of the yard, in a homemade bin, or in any number of commercially available composters.

THE RULES OF COMPOSTING

The best compost piles include a fairly even mixture of carbon ("brown"—such as leaves) and nitrogen ("green"—such as grass cuttings). The success of a compost pile depends on what you put in—and, more importantly, what you leave out.

Do compost

- Deadheaded flowers, pruned soft stems, leaf litter, and grass clippings
- Eggshells
- Coffee grounds and filters, and tea bags
- Vegetable and fruit trimmings
- Shredded newspaper and paper (black and white sections only)
- Sawdust

Don't compost

- Weeds
- Bread and other baked goods
- Wrappers and packaging
- Animal fats, or chicken, beef, or fish leftovers
- Bones
- Animal poop
- Thick wood stems or branches
- Plastics
- Cheese or other dairy products
- Colored paper or paper with colored ink printing
- Fats, grease, or oils
- Charcoal ash
- Diseased plant parts

MAINTAINING A COMPOST PILE

Compost piles need just a little regular maintenance to break down as quickly and efficiently as possible.

Layer: Compost piles work best when they're layered with a rough balance of "green," nitrogen-heavy wet ingredients such as grass clippings, fruit and vegetable waste, and coffee grounds, and "brown," carbon-heavy dry ingredients such as shredded newspaper and leaves.

Turn: The microorganisms that break down compost ingredients need oxygen. That's why it's important to turn a compost pile with a garden fork or spade (and it's why some composters are shaped like buckets or drums and are meant to be rotated). Turn your compost at least once a week, and every other day if you want it to break down quickly. Generally, the more you turn compost, the quicker it decomposes.

Moisten: Those same beneficial microorganisms need water. Ideally, moisten your compost pile every day during dry weather. Keep it wet, but never soaking wet. Compost should be moist to the touch but should not hold together in a firm ball when you squeeze it in your hands.

Although they are easy to build, many people choose to buy small prefab compost bins like this one.

HOW TO START PLANTS

You might think that growing a garden means planting seeds, but that's not necessarily the case. There are lots of ways to start new plants. The ones you choose depend on the plant, timing, and your own preferences. No matter how you start your plants, always read seed packets, or the sticks that come with trays of seedlings or young plants in pots. It's also wise to ask a nursery professional for the best way to start a particular plant.

Seeds: This is the most common way to start plants. Seeds are inexpensive and let you get a jump on the season by planting indoors in the spring before garden soil is warm enough for young plants. Seed packets list essential growing information, including sun exposure, zones, the depth to plant the seeds, and other specifics. You can start seeds in just about any container as long as it is clean and drains properly. Use fresh potting soil and keep seeds moist and in their preferred sun exposure or under a grow light. Feed growing seeds liquid fertilizer as soon as their first growth appears to start the plants off right. Keep in mind that some plants are incredibly difficult to start from seed. That's why you may not be able to find seeds for some of the plants you choose—but you'll probably be able to find seedlings, potted starts, or other forms of the plant for your garden.

Nursery seedling trays: If you or your parents are willing the spend the money, buy seedlings when you're ready to plant to simplify the process. Starting plants this way means your choices are more limited than what you would find as seeds, however. You have to be a smart shopper with buying seedlings. They shouldn't be overly tall with measly leaves, or flopping over. The soil should be moist rather than dry, and the plants should not be brown or yellow, but a vibrant, healthy green.

Potted plants: Some types of plants, such as those that don't bloom or bear fruit until their second year, are sold in individual pots ranging from quart to gallon sizes. Inspect these plants to ensure there is no disease or other problems with the plant, no obviously dead stems, or other signs of poor plant health. Follow the instructions included on the identification stick in the pot.

GARDEN JARGON

Seedlings started inside can't necessarily be planted immediately right out in the garden. Most require *hardening off*. This is the process of introducing seedlings to greater temperature variations outside by moving them out into the garden during the day and bringing them inside after the sun goes down.

"Bare root" plants are one of the most common ways gardeners start roses in their gardens.

Bare root: It sounds strange, but some plants are sold completely without soil. Roses, for example, are often sold in bare-root form. These are meant to be planted immediately. Put them in a container or a garden bed following the planting instructions—most importantly, the depth of planting. A lot of bare-root plants will only thrive if their crown is placed right above soil level.

Cuttings: This is a way to grow a new plant from an existing one. The original plant must be healthy. The cutting is taken from a green, new stem with at least one node and healthy new leaves on it. Use clean scissors or pruners to cut right above the node, leaving a stem at least 4 to 6 inches (10 to 15 cm) long. Have an adult use an precision knife or razor blade to slice through the node. Dip that end into water mixed with rooting hormone and then plant it in potting soil. Cover it with plastic and leave it in a sunlit area, watering whenever the soil dries out.

Division: As with cuttings, this is a way to get more plants from those you already have. Only certain plants can be divided, and those that can should be divided regularly to keep them healthy and growing. Division involves digging plants up. That will reveal a cluster of roots, rhizomes, bulbs, or bulblets. Separate the group with a shovel, knife, or by pulling them apart; then replant the divisions and the original.

HOW TO GROW SEEDLINGS IN AN EGG CARTON

WHAT YOU'LL NEED

CARDBOARD EGG CARTON

POTTING SOIL

COFFEE GROUNDS

PLASTIC BUCKET

SEEDS

SCISSORS

WATERING CAN

This is a fantastic way to get seeds off to a great start and get ahead of the planting season. As a bonus, you'll be recycling a cardboard egg carton.

1 Save a cardboard egg carton or cartons for your seedlings. Use only cardboard egg cartons for this project because Styrofoam cartons will not properly break down, and they could release harmful chemicals into the soil.

2 Mix 1 part used coffee grounds to 3 parts potting soil in a bucket or large coffee can. (Have your parents save all their coffee grounds because those are great additions to the soil in your garden.)

3 Use a spoon or scoop to fill each egg cup in the carton with the soil mix. Poke a hole in the center of the mix and drop in the seed (some plants should be started with several seeds in the same hole; read the instructions on the seed packet).

4 Put the egg carton on a plastic tray or sheet in a place where it will receive direct sun during much of the day. Lightly water the seeds once a day.

5 When the seedlings sprouts, thin out as recommended on the seed packet. As soon as the seedlings have two sets of leaves, they are ready to be planted outside. If the weather hasn't yet completely warmed, "harden off" the seedlings by placing them outside in a sunny location during the day and bringing them in at night.

6 When you're ready to plant the seedlings, moisten the entire egg carton, and then cut each cup free. Plant individual cups according to the spacing recommended on the seed packet. Make sure the soil around the seedling in the ground or container matches the level of the seed cup soil.

GARDEN JARGON

There is a science for just about every growing thing and that includes growing vegetables. The science of vegetable gardening (technically including the harvesting, storage, and sale of vegetables) is called *olericulture*.

HOW TO FIGHT PESTS & DISEASES

Grow your garden right and it's a wonderful environment for all kinds of life. Unfortunately, that includes garden pests and diseases that are just part of nature. Here are the most common problems home gardeners deal with and the best solutions for getting rid of them. If you're puzzled by a bug or a disease affecting your plants and can't figure out what it is, you can take a sample to your local County Extension Service office and the professionals there will identify it for you. No matter what, though, don't use chemical pesticides on or around edible plants. It's also best for your garden's long-term health to avoid introducing harsh chemicals.

PESTS

Aphids: These tiny critters feed on a plant's sap, sucking it out of leaves and stems, and leaving yellowed and dying plant parts behind. These tiny, quarter-inch (6 mm), pear-shaped insects cluster together in groups and leave behind a sticky coating.

Aphids

SOLUTION: The most natural way to solve your aphid problem is to introduce beneficial insects that eat them—ladybugs, lacewings, and parasitic wasps. If you only have a few aphids, you may be able to blast them off the plant with the spray from a hose. More established groups can be treated with a healthy dose of insecticidal soap following the instructions on the bottle.

Beetles: There are many types of garden beetles but only a few attack plants. Most, like the Japanese beetle, are easy to see, as is the damage they do. Beetle *grubs* are sneakier, living in the soil and attacking plant roots.

SOLUTION: The easiest way to eliminate beetles is to remove them by hand into a sealed bag. Protect plants with floating row covers or netting or set out beetle traps following the directions on the box. You can also spray beetles with insecticidal soap. You can get rid of grubs by spraying beneficial nematodes or Neem oil (these will usually take multiple applications). Put up a wren birdhouse and the birds may take care of the problem for you!

Earwigs: Sometimes called "pincher bugs," earwigs are brown or black, between ¼ to 1 inch (.6 to 2.5 cm) long, with pinchers on their backside. Earwigs love moisture and will gladly eat just about any part of a plant.

SOLUTION: Remove any rotting wood or standing water. You can make your own earwig traps by filling a small plastic container with a lid with soy sauce and canola oil and punching holes in the lid big enough for earwigs to crawl through. Dig small holes and bury the containers so that the lid is at soil level. Add more traps wherever you see earwig activity and regularly check and empty the traps. You can also put rings of diatomaceous earth around the base of affected plants.

Hornworm

Stinkbug

Hornworms: These horned, light green caterpillars look a little bit like a rolled-up leaf, making them hard to detect. They eat stems and leaves and particularly like tomato plants.

SOLUTION: If there are only one or two, it's easy to hand-pick and remove the pests. A blast of water on a plant's leaves will reveal any hornworms. For more serious cases, use Bt (*Bacillus thuringiensis*), an organic biological pesticide that is safe for food crops and can also be used to treat other caterpillars (follow the directions on the label).

Spider mites: These are teeny, tiny pests that may be red or brown and look like spiders under a magnifying glass. They suck the sap out of leaves and will eventually kill all or part of a plant. You'll find large clusters of them on the undersides of leaves, combined with yellow and dead leaves.

SOLUTION: The best solution is to introduce beneficial insects that will quickly feed on the mites. Remove and bag affected leaves. In the worst cases, use a food-grade organic insecticide.

Slugs and snails: These slimy crawlers are easy to see, as is the damage the do. They love to eat the tender parts of plants. The good news is that they move slowly and there are a number of ways to stop them.

SOLUTION: Surround susceptible plants such as seedlings with a ring of coffee grounds or sawdust. Crushed eggshells also work, as will diatomaceous earth. A good slug trap can be made from a deep saucer of stale beer set out near where you see slug tracks. The slugs will be attracted to the beer and will drown in the saucer.

Stinkbugs: Depending on where in the country you live, these brown, triangular, ¾-inch (2 cm)-long bugs may be a real problem in the garden and even in your home. Originally from Asia, they reproduce very quickly and are prolific, and they give off a disgusting stink when crushed. They feed on stems, leaves, and fruit.

SOLUTION: The best way to fight this pest is by hand-picking them (wearing gloves) and dropping them in a bucket of hot, soapy water. You can also spray them with Neem oil or insecticidal soap.

Thrips: Thrips are tiny, whitish yellow insects that look like grains of rice and will eat plant leaves, killing them. Even if you don't see the thrips, you may detect their damage to leaves and see their telltale black spots.

SOLUTION: Remove damaged leaves and unopened buds with thrips or thrips damage and throw them in the garbage. You can also spray with insecticidal soap or Neem oil.

Whiteflies: These look exactly like their name suggests, tiny, pure white winged insects that suck a plant's sap by feeding on the undersides of leaves.

SOLUTION: Put out yellow sticky traps at the first sign of whiteflies. You can also blast them off plants with a hose or introduce beneficial insects such as lacewings. If the infestation is more severe, use insecticidal soap or Neem oil.

Beneficial Insects

Just because you notice insects in your garden doesn't mean you necessarily have a problem. In fact, sometimes you may have a solution and don't even know it! There is a group of insects that help in your garden. Some pollinate flowers while others prey on garden pests, keeping your plants safe. These insects are a good reason for not using pesticides in a garden, and you can actually purchase these from some nurseries.

Aphid midge: As its name implies, this tiny flylike insect attacks aphids.

Braconid wasps: Don't swat this small wasp; left alone it will gladly attack aphids and caterpillars for you. (It actually plants eggs on caterpillars including tomato hornworms. The eggs then feed on the caterpillars.)

Damsel bugs: These tiny green insects prey on a host of garden pests, including caterpillars, aphids, mites, and cabbage worms.

Lacewings: It can be easy to mistake a lacewing for a whitefly, but that would be a mistake. Lacewings actually prey on whiteflies, as well as aphids, leafhoppers, and mealybugs.

Ladybugs: These are the most adorable insects you'll encounter in your garden, but that doesn't make them any less deadly to garden pests. Adult ladybugs and their larvae feed on some of the most persistent garden pests, including aphids and mealybugs.

Braconid wasp

Lacewing

DISEASES

Blights: This is a plant-destroying fungus. You'll first notice blight on older leaves, as brown, dry spots. Early treatment is important to stop the fungus from spreading.

SOLUTION: Remove and destroy affected plant parts (that includes leaves on the ground). To head off blights, water plants at ground level and don't splash the stems or leaves. If it persists, use a food-safe copper-based fungicide dust on your plants, following the directions on the label.

Blossom end rot: A disease that affects young tomatoes, peppers, and squash, this rot appears on the young fruit and quickly makes it inedible before it can mature. It's caused by a lack of calcium in the soil or improper watering.

SOLUTION: Unfortunately once it appears, blossom end rot is almost impossible to fix. The best solution is to amend soils before planting vegetables to ensure the soil is rich in calcium. Then use a drip-irrigation system or go by a strict schedule to keep the soil moist but not soaking wet.

Molds and mildews: These are fungi that all create similar symptoms: white or black spots that left untreated will grow to cover the leaves, then the stems of the plant.

SOLUTION: There are lots of natural, easy treatments for molds and mildews. Take action as soon as you detect the condition. A spray made of a teaspoon of baking soil and a teaspoon of vegetable oil mixed with a quart of water in a spray bottle, sprayed on the leaves once every couple of days, will fix the problem. You can also water down whole milk and spray that on the plant. Vinegar will also work in many cases, but it has to be diluted to avoid burning the plant. Mix 1 teaspoon of vinegar in 1 quart (946 ml) of warm water and spray it on the plant every day for a week.

Rust: Rust is the result of a fungal parasite and can spread from affected plants to healthy ones by way of spores. The disease appears as small white spots early on, and large orange-brown raised bumps later.

SOLUTION: Rust is difficult to fight once it's established. Remove any plant part that is affected and remove entire plants if necessary. Prevent rust by dusting plants with sulfur early in the season, being careful to give plants plenty of room to allow for air circulation.

Lastly, protect your garden from four-legged and winged "pests." Deer, raccoons, and other wildlife steal fruits and vegetables, and birds will feast on certain fruit. Protect plants with wire fencing and use bird netting to protect vulnerable fruits such as blueberry bushes.

Blight

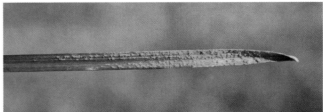

Rust

4 GREAT BED GARDENS

Garden beds are often the easiest and quickest option for gardeners. Putting your plants right in the garden soil means you don't have work with containers or build anything. Bed gardens usually also give the opportunity to grow a bigger garden than you otherwise would have. That means you can grow great big crops of edibles or cut flowers to fill the house every week of the summer (or plant a mix of both!).

The number-one consideration is the state of the soil. Test the soil (page 19) to make sure it is in good shape and ready to give your plants everything they need. Amend it as needed, but it's also wise to add a balanced amendment such as compost no matter what.

Think carefully about where you plant things. Although it is easiest to place one type of plant in a row or next to one another, clustering the same plant in one place makes insect and disease spread more likely. Mix up plant locations and it can be a little difficult to tell what's what until they mature, but it can lead to better overall plant health.

The downside to planting gardens in the ground is the hated enemy of all gardeners—weeds. Nobody likes weeding. But it's important that weeds do not grow unrestricted or they will steal nutrients and root space from the plants you choose for your garden. You can head off a lot of weeding by using mulch, such as shredded pine bark, around the base of your plants. Just be sure to leave a ring of soil between the mulch and each plant stem to avoid problems.

QUESTIONS THIS CHAPTER ANSWERS

- What are the different types of garden beds? Is one better than the others?
- What plants should you avoid?
- How do you set up a basic bed garden? What are the secrets to success?
- What is a cut-flower garden and what type of plants do you grow there?
- How does where you live affect the sun exposure your garden receives?
- What are the best plants to make a garden smell nice?

GARDEN BED TYPES

There are two basic types of garden beds: in-ground beds and raised beds. Each has pros and cons.

In-ground beds: These can be much larger than raised beds, which means you can grow much more produce in a vegetable garden or many more types of flowers in a flower bed. Although they can be a mix of plants, most gardeners dedicate a garden bed to either edibles or "ornamentals"—plants grown just for their looks. That makes taking care of the plants in any one bed much easier.

Vegetable garden beds are traditionally grown as "row gardens." The gardener uses a hoe to created straight trenches, "furrows," or sometimes mounds soil in "hills" that create natural furrows between the rows. Flower beds are typically less structured and are designed with the tallest flowers at the back of the bed and the smallest along the front.

The challenge with any in-ground garden is that you have less control than you do with a raised bed or a container garden. The soil may need to be periodically improved, and it's harder to protect in-ground gardens from pests such as pets and wildlife. You may even have to deal with underground pests, such as gophers or moles.

Raised-bed gardens: These are all about making gardening easier. Once you've built the bed, you control the soil that goes into it and the plants are in a more restricted space, which makes tending to them easier. Raised beds also allow you to garden in spaces where you otherwise couldn't, such as on top of a concrete patio. The downside is that the space you have to work with is limited, and you can't really plant things that grow deep, such as potatoes. You'll find more information on working with raised beds in chapter 5.

A basic row garden is a way to raise all the produce your family might eat over a summer.

Raised beds are a way to keep the garden nice and tidy and contained.

Dangerous Plants

Garden plants can be powerful. Many contain compounds in their flowers, leaves, stems, or seeds that have medicinal uses. But those same compounds can make the plant deadly to ingest. Many common garden plants, such as rhododendron, azaleas, and daffodils, are poisonous if eaten and can you make sick. Certain ones, though, are downright deadly and **should not** be included in home gardens. Here's a partial list:

Belladonna (*Atropa belladonna*): Appropriately named "deadly nightshade," belladonna is an attractive shrub with light purple flowers and black berries. The berries have been used by medical professionals through history but eating the berries or flowers can make a child or pet incredibly sick.

Caster bean (*Ricinus communis*): The large-growing caster bean plant looks strange and beautiful. It has weird bean pods, frilly red flowers, and gigantic, dark leaves. Oil from the plant has medicinal uses. Unfortunately, the seeds—or "beans"—can be deadly. They are as pretty as the flowers, which makes them attractive to small children. Sadly, the seeds contain the deadly toxin ricin. Eating one can quickly kill a child.

Foxglove (*Digitalis purpurea*): This biennial plant is one of the prettiest in nature. Tall stems hold spires of flowers. But those flowers hold a dangerous secret. Foxglove is the source for a heart medication called digitalis. But the same compound that makes this a medicinal plant can make it a killer if the beautiful flowers or berries are consumed. Small children and pets are attracted to foxglove's blooms, which is why is shouldn't be grown in home gardens.

Oleander (*Nerium oleander*): This gorgeous shrub displays flashy pink flowers. But its good looks hide a deadly nature. Although the plant has been used to develop treatments for illnesses from malaria to leprosy, every part of the shrub is poisonous if eaten. Even honey from bees that have pollinated it is toxic.

Belladonna

PREP AND PLANT A ROW GARDEN

WHAT YOU'LL NEED

MEASURING TAPE

LIME OR LANDSCAPER'S PAINT

WOOD STAKES

TWINE OR STRING

SHOVEL

PICK (OPTIONAL)

HOE

TROWEL

AMENDMENTS (OPTIONAL)

SEEDS OR SEEDLINGS

Row gardens have been used to grow vegetables for thousands of years. That's because they are easy to create, plant, and tend. The basic idea couldn't be simpler: create trenches—called furrows—or raised rows, so that watering is easy (at its most basic, you can just flood the furrows), as is weeding, because you know exactly where you planted your crops.

Row gardens are usually only used to grow single-season vegetables because growing trees, shrubs, or perennials in a row garden wouldn't make a lot of sense. Gardeners usually grow a single type of plant in each row, but that's not a hard-and-fast rule. It does make tending the garden easier, but it also makes the spread of disease and insect pests more likely. You can mix up the type of plants you put in any one row but be careful to use the spacing recommended on the seed packet or seedling tray tags.

1

1 Measure and mark out the garden plot with string or by using landscaping paint or lime. Dig up the garden plot to a depth of about 4 inches (10 cm). Rake the surface smooth, breaking up and large dirt clods, and remove large rocks. Or, you can dig in any amendments that you need to add to the garden plot, and level the surface of the soil with a rake. This will require digging deeper to integrate the amendment.

2 Check your seed packets or talk to a nursery professional about the plants you want to grow to determine the proper spacing they'll need. Measure and place a stake in the ground at the end of each row.

3 Stretch twine or string between the stakes, tying it to the stakes at either end of a row. Use the string as a guide for digging out the furrow as shown here (or for mounding raised rows, if you prefer that method).

4 Hoe along the twine in each row to create the planting furrow. Mark the planting location for each type of vegetable along the rows with a plant marker (which can be homemade).

5 Plant all your plants in the marked rows. Lightly water all the furrows. Lay down a layer of mulch to conserve moisture and prevent weeds.

2

4

GROW A COLORFUL CUT-FLOWER GARDEN

A cut-flower garden is a double pleasure. Not only will you and your family enjoy a multicolored display in your yard, you'll be able to cut flowers and arrange them in combinations of shapes and colors (and, in some cases, fragrance) that appeal most to you to decorate your house. Even better, bouquets of cut flowers make fantastic gifts for someone like Grandma.

Choose the right flowers and they will be low-maintenance, fast-growing, and prolific bloomers. The ideal candidates grow flowers on long stems, last all summer long, and tend to increase flower production as you cut the ones that are already blooming. Beyond that, you'll get the most enjoyment if you plant lots of different shapes, sizes, and colors.

WHAT YOU'LL NEED

MEASURING TAPE

SHOVEL OR GARDEN SPADE

TROWEL

RAKE

PLANTS OR SEEDS

SOIL AMENDMENTS (OPTIONAL)

GRANULAR FERTILIZER (OPTIONAL)

MULCH

CUT-FLOWER GARDEN TIPS

Use a few simple techniques to get the most out of any cut-flower garden you plant.

- Plant in stages—one plant or variety early, another a week later, and so on—to have flowers continuously from late May through September.
- Regularly deadhead cut-flower plants. Deadheading is the practice of pinching off or cutting off faded blooms, so that the plant puts more energy into new blooms.
- Use clean, sharp pruning shears when cutting your flowers. Raggedly cut stems can make the plant susceptible to disease.

The Science of Preserving Cut Flowers

Cut flowers are just a temporary pleasure. But there are ways of increasing how long they will last in a vase. It's all about how cut flowers take up water.

Even though they've been cut from their plant, flowers aren't dead yet. Think of it as if a human has a finger cut off. Those cells don't die right away, and if the deterioration of the cells is slowed down by chilling (which is why you put a severed digit in a bag of ice to preserve it), the body part can possibly be reattached and revived with new blood flow.

That means the secret to helping cut flowers last as long as possible is to ensure that they get nutrients and water they would as if the flowers were still on the plant. That's why you should put cut flowers in room temperature water as soon as possible after cutting them. To aid in the capillary action (see page 22), by which flowers draw up water, recut their cut ends under running water before putting them in a vase.

Just as important is what's in the water in the vase. Remember, flowers need energy to keep blooming. For a plant, that means sugar. Adding a little powdered sugar—which will dissolve quicker in water than granulated sugar—will increase the length of time cut flowers stay fresh. But you also have to protect the cut flower's cells from microbes in the water. That's why an antimicrobial is important and why a lot of people add a capful of bleach to vase water. A tablespoon of white vinegar will be just as effective (the acid in the vinegar will kill microbes in the water).

And just as putting a severed finger on ice helps its cells live a little longer, putting a vase of flowers in the refrigerator before you go to bed and taking them out in the morning will slow the deterioration of a flower's cells and keep your bouquet looking beautiful longer.

1 Pick a location for your cut-flower garden bed. Measure it and double-check the site's sun exposure. (Your blooms will be disappointing if you misjudge and there is too little sun.)

2 Choose your plants from a catalog, seed rack, or the nursery (see the Cut-Flower Garden Superstars sidebar on page 83). Dig up the bed to a depth of 4 inches (10 cm). Add any amendments the soil needs and dig those into the bed. Rake the bed level, breaking up any dirt clods.

3 Begin laying out the seedlings or potted plants in position. If you're planting seeds, use small plastic plant pots placed upside-down to represent the positions of the plants. Double-check the plant spacings before planting anything.

4

4 "Edit" the plant layout. Measure the distance between plants to be sure they have enough room when they're mature (remember, proper air circulation is key to preventing diseases), and leave some room to get to plants so that you can cut the blooms. However, don't be afraid to move the border plants—the shorter-growing types at the front—closer than recommended to the front of the bed. It's okay if flowers are spilling out the front.

5 Plant your cut-flower choices. If you want to get your flowers off to the best start, add a little granular fertilizer or compost to the hole before dropping in the seed or planting the seedling.

6

6 Water the garden bed thoroughly. Spread a layer of mulch at least 2 inches (5 cm) thick around the plants. The mulch should not be touching or covering any part of a seedling or plant stem.

5

9 CUT-FLOWER GARDEN SUPERSTARS

Some flowers are just better than others for cutting. The good news is, there are so many potential cut-flower garden possibilities that you can plant a wonderful mix of forms, including spiky, round, fluffy, and more. Of course, you'll also choose from a rainbow's worth of colors! Here are nine of the best.

Aster (*Astereae*): Unlike many cut-flower plants, asters are perennials. The daisylike flowers grow in shades or red, pink, purple, and blue with gold centers.

Daisy: There are many kinds of daisies, but the one most people think of when they hear the name is the bright white *Shasta daisy* (*Leucanthemum × superbum*). However, just about any daisy will make a wonderful addition to your cut-flower garden and the other species come in a multitude of fun colors.

Dahlia: A classic cut-flower choice, dahlias grow lots and lots of rounded flowers packed with layers of tight petals. They grow in just about any color you can imagine.

Delphinium: This perennial grows spikes of small flowers that create a wonderfully unusual look in a vase. The flowers come in blues, pinks, purples, and white. As a bonus, the flowers attract butterflies.

Calendula: Calendula plants really pack the blooms onto their bushy form, and the flowers can be eaten or used to make a tea that many people believe has medicinal benefits. The flowers have a form like a daisy and come in shades of yellow, gold, and white.

Cosmos: Cosmos are yet another flower shaped like a daisy with large petals in shades of pink, red, and white with gold centers. They have long, spindly stems that makes them ideal for tall vase arrangements.

Liatris (*Liatris spicata*): Sometimes sold as "blazing star," this garden stunner grows bunches of deep purple flowers on skinny stems. The flowers attract bees and butterflies as well as other beneficial insects.

Speedwell (*Veronica*): Another perennial that is loved by gardeners for its spiky, brightly colored flower clusters in tones of blue, pink, and white is speedwell. It grows lower to the ground than other cut-flower species, but it is tough and low-maintenance.

Zinnias: This classic cut flower is a sturdy performer all summer and is extremely rugged and easy to grow. The flowers come in a fantastic range of colors and forms, with the flowers topping long, slender stems.

Dahlia

Delphinium

Liatris

RAISE A
SCENTED BORDER

Scented plants are ideal for a border garden along a pathway, patio, deck, or even a stretch of grass. As people pass by the plants, they'll catch the fragrances, adding yet another pleasing element to a flower garden. Cut the flowers from a scented border and they can fill a house with their incredible fragrances.

Even as lovely as most scented plants are, not everyone loves every scented plant. It's always smart to head to a local botanical garden or a large nursery to check out mature versions of any plants you're considering for your scented border. That way, you can ensure that you'll grow the fragrances that appeal to you the most (and avoid any you find less than pleasant!).

Many of these plants are perennials, so plant scented borders carefully. When you get them right, they will be a treasured part of your garden for years to come.

1 Fill a measuring cup or other container with a spout (such as an empty milk container) with lime. Define the front edge of the border by laying a line of the lime. You can also use landscaping paint (available at home centers and nurseries), colored string, or even a hose.

4 Install any edging you are using for the border. Make sure it is either secured in a trench, tapped down into the soil (as with the edging shown in this photo), or staked in place. This is optional, but for a more elaborate, decorative edging such as stacked rock or slanted brick, dig out a flat-bottomed trench the width of the edging you are using. Line the bottom of the trench with a weed barrier such as plastic sheeting, then a layer of rock, leveling it along the length of the trench. Set the stones or brick into the trench, leveling them as you go.

2 Use a garden spade to dig out the edge to a depth of about 8 inches (20 cm). Move carefully along the line of lime from one end to the other, putting one point into the soil and then stepping on the blade to drive the shovel in following the marked line.

3 Dig out the grass and debris on the inside of the marked line. Lightly turn over the soil and rake out the surface to remove any grass, weeds, rock, or yard debris like leaves. Amend the soil as necessary and rake it level.

5

5 Plant the scented plants, with taller varieties at the back of the border. Don't be afraid to put plants right up to the edging so that they grow over it. They will be brushed as people walk by them.

6 Water the border thoroughly, and mulch with shredded bark.

The Sun's Path

You probably know that the Sun rises in the east and sets in the west. Because America is located north of the equator—the line that marks the middle of the Earth—the Sun is strongest to our south. (If the morning sun is to your left, that's east, so the direction you're facing is south.) That's why the farther you go north in our hemisphere (or any part of the globe), the colder it gets—you're moving away from the Sun.

If you've watched the path of the Sun or noticed sunlight through a window in different seasons, you'll know that the Sun is lower in the sky in the winter than the summer. That's because the North Pole of the Earth is always pointed toward the fixed point of the North Star. That creates a 23.5-degree tilt in the axis at all points, so the hemisphere we're in leans farther from the Sun during winter and closer to the Sun in summer. Although it's Earth that's moving, that makes it appear as if the Sun is traveling a different path in different seasons. That tilt also accounts for why it's hotter in summer and colder in winter (it's like leaning closer to or farther from a fire).

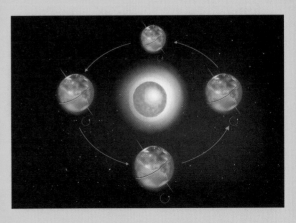

THE 10 BEST SCENTED FLOWERING PLANTS

There are many scented plants that will do your garden proud. In addition to plants that are naturally fragrant, many otherwise odorless annuals have scented varieties, such as chocolate cosmos. Several interesting scented plants require warmer climates; if you live in zones 8–11, the options will be even greater—such as moonflower, which releases its scent at night. Don't forget that most herbs are aromatic too. Rosemary or mint can do double duty in a scented border—nice fragrances and great cooking accents!

Jasmine (*Jasminum floridum*): There are other species of jasmine that aren't scented, but this one smells like a clean, fresh perfume. The aroma attracts pollinators to your garden, while gardeners enjoy the shrub form and its delicate yellow flowers are attractive to people. Star jasmine is a scented perennial vine that works well at the back of a scented border trained up a wall or fence. It isn't really a true jasmine (it's *Trachelospermum jasminoides*), but it smells wonderful just the same. Zones 7–10.

Geranium (*Pelargonium*): Grown as an annual in most places, geraniums give off a distinctive dusky scent. These low-growing plants are excellent at the front or middle of a scented border to fill in bare areas. There are many specifically scented varieties, in aromas of pineapple, lemon, chocolate, and more.

Heliotrope (*Heliotropium arborescens*): The name translates from Greek to the words "sun" and "turn"; in fact, the flowerheads do turn to face the Sun. This bushy sun lover will grow as a perennial in the hottest zones but is usually grown as an annual for its stunning purple or white flower clusters and cherry pie aroma.

Lavender (*Lavandula*): The low-growing bushy form and gray-green leaves of this heat-loving perennial is attractive in their own right, but the abundance of purple or blue flowers on straw-thin stems adds stunning form and color to any border. Its scent is mild but pleasant, and the flowers can be used fresh or dried to lend a clean fragrance to linens or flavor to baked goods.

Lilac (*Syringa*): A beautiful shrub, lilac blooms in clusters of blue, purple, pink, red, white, or yellow flowers. They give off a perfume scent that adds a lovely element to any scented border. This shrub also attracts butterflies and pollinators. Zones 2–7.

Jasmine

Pinks

Stock

Pinks (*Dianthus*): The stunning flowers of perennial dianthus cover the plant's rounded, low-growing form adding a cascade of pink, white, red, or light purple flowers to the front of a scented border. Pinks give off a light spicy clove aroma. Zones 3–9.

Phlox: One of the most versatile scented border options, phlox includes varieties that bloom blue, pink, purple, red, or white, and forms that range from groundcovers to shrubs. The shrub can tolerate shade and attracts both birds and butterflies. It has a light, pleasant aroma. Zones 2–9.

Rose: Not every rose is scented, but the ones that are offer unforgettable fresh perfumed aromas that bring a lot of appeal to a scented border. Unfortunately, roses need space and proper air circulation to grow disease-free, so they may not be right for a dense shrub border. But where they fit in, the range of possible colors and blooming periods, along with the long-lasting nature of this perennial, make this a good scented border choice. Zones 2–10.

Stock (*Matthiola incana*): This fast-growing annual blooms with thick flower clusters in just about every color in the spectrum. They make wonderful cut flowers with a zingy, clove-like scent.

Sweet Alyssum (*Lobularia maritima*): This annual is a favorite to fill in the front of borders will its little mounded forms covered in purple or white flowers. It has a light, sweet, refreshing aroma and will tolerate full sun to partial shade.

5

HANDY CONTAINER GARDENING

Containers are a great way for any gardener to grow plants but particularly for those with space constraints or other garden limitations. It may be that your parents just want to keep the backyard lawn undisturbed, or maybe your backyard is too small and shady to grow a garden. Containers are the answer because you control the environment. You can supply exactly the soil type and water that any individual plant needs, and you place it in precisely the perfect sun exposure.

Containers do, however, have their limitations. The first and most obvious is the size. Even with multiple containers, you can only grow a limited garden. Some plants don't like to be raised in containers and will not do well in one. You have to be careful when choosing container garden plants that you plan for the mature sizes of the plants. If a plant is too crowded in the container, its roots will become rootbound and will stop growing, and so will the plant.

Containers also require a fair amount of diligence. With the help of an adult, you can set up an automatic watering setup, like a drip-irrigation system. Otherwise, you will have to water your containers regularly to ensure that are getting the proper amount of hydration.

But do it right and container gardening can be a way to have beautiful or edible plants right out on the back patio or deck. Containers will also allow you to bring sensitive perennials inside over winter—which may be the only way to ensure that they survive.

QUESTIONS THIS CHAPTER ANSWERS

- What are the best edibles and herbs to grow in a container?
- How do you ensure proper drainage in a container garden?
- How deep should you plant bulbs in a pot or other container?
- What kind of recycled containers can you use for container gardening?

POT A KITCHEN GARDEN

WHAT YOU'LL NEED

TROWEL

ROCK OR BROKEN TERRACOTTA

PLANT POTS

CORDLESS DRILL AND BITS

ASSORTMENT OF HERB SEEDLINGS,
OR DWARF VARIETIES OF YOUR
FAVORITE VEGETABLES

POTTING SOIL MIX

Fresh herbs are luxury in any kitchen. Whether your mom or dad does all the cooking or you try your hand at whipping up dinner, having fresh herbs on hand will make everything taste a little bit better. The best part? Growing this garden is as easy as pie. Once you get plants established, you'll just need to check on them every couple of days to ensure they have enough water and that no pests are trying to move in on your bounty.

1 Choose a location where the herbs will get at least 6 hours of sun a day. Ideally, the location should be close to the back door or a door leading to a deck or patio. A south- or east-facing orientation will be best.

2 Make sure the containers you are using are clean; it's important not to transmit soilborne diseases from one container plant to the next. If the pot is plastic with a solid bottom, drill several ¼-inch (.6-cm) holes in the bottom for drainage. (Have your mom or dad drill the holes if you're not allowed to handle power tools.)

Gardening without Soil

Although it hardly seems possible, you don't actually have to have soil to grow a garden. In fact, a whole branch of horticulture, called *hydroponics*, is dedicated to getting the most from plants without ever putting them in soil. This involves immersing the roots in a nutrient-rich water that carries all the minerals and compounds the plant would normally get from soil. As the plant takes up water, it takes up the nutrients in the water. This allows horticulturists to grow plants in places where the soil is either inhospitable to the crops people want to grow, or in places far from soil (like in the upper floors of a building). A similar science called *aeroponics* focuses growing plants by misting their roots with the nutrient-rich water.

3 Add a shallow layer of stones or broken terracotta pieces to the bottom of each pot to aid drainage and help keep the containers from tipping over. Add potting soil up to the rim; don't tamp it down.

4 Make small "pockets" in the soil of each container for the plants. Drench the plants' rootballs in a bucket half full of water, and then firm the plants down in the mix in the containers.

5 Place each container in its final location in saucers that are the correct size for each container. Thoroughly water each container or set up a drip-irrigation system for all the containers.

MOTHER'S DAY FORCED TULIPS IN A BOX

WHAT YOU'LL NEED

TROWEL

OLD CRATE WITH SOLID BOTTOM AND SIDES (OR AN ANTIQUE TIN CONTAINER)

RED TULIP BULBS (10-INCH VARIETY)

POTTING SOIL MIX

LANDSCAPING FABRIC

STAPLE GUN AND STAPLES (OPTIONAL)

For an extra special gift, "force" tulips in an unusual container, like the box in this project. You could use an antique cookie tin or other container that you think your mom (or grandma) would like. The one requirement is that it be able to drain, so that the bulbs aren't kept wet and eventually rot.

1 Set up on a workbench or other uncluttered surface that will be easy to clean. If the box has slats, line the box with the landscaping fabric or even black trash bag plastic to contain the soil. Staple the fabric to the sides all around.

2 Spread a thin layer of potting soil on the bottom of the box. Set the tulip bulbs in place, tips up, crowding them next to one another (the idea is to create a stunning display, so the more bulbs, the better). Disregard any spacing requirements on the tulip package.

3 Pack in potting soil around the bulbs, up to their tips. Don't overly compact the soil, but make sure it is firm enough to hold the bulbs securely.

4 Slip the box into a black garbage bag and place the box into a refrigerator (not a freezer). Remove the box 7 weeks before Mother's Day, and keep the box on a warm and sunny windowsill, watering it regularly. Loosely wrap the stems in a ribbon and put a bow on the box when you're ready to give it to your mother or another loved one.

GARDEN JARGON

Forcing is the artificial process of tricking bulbs to flower indoors and out of season. You can force just about any bulb, and it's a wonderful way of having beautiful, brightly colored flowers in the dead of winter. You can force bulbs in soil, gravel, or even in water in special "forcing jars" or containers. Normally, when forcing a bulb in soil, the soil should be at least twice as deep as the bulb height. Keep the bulb refrigerated until you're ready to start growing the flower. Then take it out and transfer to whatever container you're using. Keep it in full sun, in a warm area of the house. It will bloom according to the regular flowering time for that bulb.

Naturalizing is almost the exact opposite of forcing. Although some bulbs should be dug up after their foliage dies back and stored in a cool, dark place (such as a refrigerator or cellar), many can be left in the ground to bloom year after year. When the bulbs are left in place, they become naturalized.

GROW STRAWBERRIES IN A 5-GALLON BUCKET

Strawberries are often grown in special "strawberry pots" to protect them from pests and diseases and ensure that the plants grow as much of their precious fruit as possible. The problem is, strawberry pots tend to be pretty expensive.

That's not your problem, though. You can use a recycled 5-gallon bucket to create your very own strawberry pot. Five-gallon PVC buckets are easy to find and reuse because so many materials are packed and shipped in these buckets. Stores often throw them away. Chances are, you may be able to find some free ones or your parents may even have a couple in the shed or garage.

It's important to avoid buckets that have contained toxic substances, such as those that carried chemicals used to maintain pools. Try to figure out what the bucket held before or spend a couple of bucks to buy a brand-new bucket at the local hardware store or home improvement center. If you don't know what the used bucket contained before you got it, don't use it as a container in which to grow edibles.

Strawberries aren't the only things that can be grown in a 5-gallon bucket. Herbs, annual flowers, and even radishes can be planted in the bucket as it is fabricated for this project. You can also make the bucket your own by decorating the outside with paint or stencils. Just make sure you don't get any paint inside where the soil and plant roots will go. Decorating a bucket will always be easier before you start fabricating and planting it.

WHAT YOU'LL NEED

POWER DRILL AND BITS

2-INCH (5 CM) HOLE SAW BIT

MEASURING TAPE

MARKER

HANDSAW

SCISSORS

5-GALLON BUCKET

3-INCH (7.5 CM) PVC PIPE

LANDSCAPING FABRIC

STONES OR BROKEN POTTERY SHARDS

POTTING SOIL

STRAWBERRY PLANTS

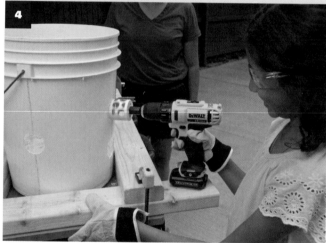

3 Use a level to draw four straight vertical lines spaced evenly around the bucket. The lines should run from just under the lowest "flange" around the top of the bucket to the bottom edge.

4 Use one end of the pipe you cut to trace a series of holes on the bucket. These should be staggered so that a bottom and top hole are centered on one vertical line, and a middle hole is centered on the next, and so on. Drill the holes with a drill and hole saw bit.

1 If you're using a recycled 5-gallon bucket, clean it thoroughly (do not use any bucket that contained chemicals or toxic ingredients such as pool chemicals). Cut the PVC pipe 16 inches (40.5 cm) long using the handsaw.

2 Clamp the pipe in a vise or clamp it down to the workbench (with a waste piece of wood underneath). Use the drill to drill ¼-inch (.6-cm) holes all around the pipe in a random pattern. If you're not allowed to handle a power drill or don't feel comfortable using one, ask your mom or dad to drill the holes. Drill ⅛-inch (.3-cm) holes in the bottom of the 5-gallon bucket for drainage.

5

STRAWBERRY PLANT DEPTH

Planting strawberries isn't hard, but it has to be done right to ensure the plants don't die or fail to produce fruit. They should be planted so that the junction between the roots and the "crowns" of the plants is right at the level of the soil.

5 Use the bucket to make an outline on the landscaping fabric and use scissors to cut out the circle. Line the bottom of the bucket with the circle. Stand the PVC pipe up in the center of the bucket and add about 1 to 2 inches (2.5 to 5 cm) of rocks or broken terracotta pot shards around the base of the pipe. Add potting soil up to the lowest holes you drilled.

6 Push strawberry plants into the lowest holes, tucking them into the soil. Repeat the process in the second and third level of holes. Add soil to the top of the bucket, and plant strawberry plants around the top so that they drape over the edge. Place the bucket in a sunny spot for the growing season. Water the soil thoroughly, and then fill the PVC pipe with water.

7 Place the bucket in a sunny spot for the growing season. Water the soil thoroughly, and then fill the PVC pipe with water.

TOO DEEP

CORRECT DEPTH

TOO SHALLOW

6

6 RAISED BED BOUNTY

Raised-bed gardens are immensely popular because they can be easier to care for than in-ground beds, and they hold a lot more plants than any container garden will. The right raised-bed garden can even be placed on a solid surface such as a concrete patio, allowing you have a substantial garden where you might not be able to otherwise. A raised bed can also be used in areas, such as on top of an existing lawn, where you don't want the garden spreading out on its own.

Making this type of garden even more versatile, there are several different kinds of raised-bed gardens. You can make one any size or shape, but a 3-foot × 3-foot bed marked off in square foot increments, is the basis of the wildly popular Square Foot Gardening movement (see more about that on page 108). You can also make a raised bed extra deep to accommodate something that needs deeper space, such as potatoes.

Tiered raised-bed gardens can be fun to look at and let you create different growing environments for different sizes, shapes, and plant species. A variation of the tiered bed, the herb spiral, is a winding garden that starts at ground level and eventually rises to a small bed at the top. It's been used for decades and is not only fun to create, it can establish ideal planting conditions for many different kinds of herbs. That makes it a great way to get the most out of an herb garden.

Whichever you choose, a raised-bed garden gives you lots of control over how and what you grow. If you use an automatic watering system like drip irrigation, along with a lot of mulch, you may not even have much maintenance to do after planting the garden!

QUESTION THIS CHAPTER WILL ANSWER

- What are Square Foot Gardens? Why are they efficient for growing vegetables? How do you build one?
- How do you grow plants vertically? What are the best supports for different edibles?
- What are different types of raised-bed gardens and how do you choose one and adapt it to your needs?
- What is a herb spiral and why is it a good option for a kitchen garden?

NURTURE A SQUARE FOOT GARDEN

Square Foot Gardening is a method that was invented by engineer Mel Bartholomew. As you might imagine from him being an engineer, Mel based his system on math. The garden is evenly divided into three square feet (four square feet for the adult version) each way. Mel figured out that this is the optimum space to allow a diversity of plants while still being manageable enough that the gardener can easily reach into the center of the raised bed.

The math continues to the planting grid in each square. Mel's theory about planting the Square Foot Gardening raised bed was that because you tightly control the environment, more plants can be grown together. Different plants have different spacing in each square foot, but they are meant to be kept the same space from one another and the sides of the square. (See opposite for specific plant spacing requirements.)

Tending a Square Foot Garden is supposed to be as easy as possible. Because the area is so small, you water when the plants need it, by hand. (Author Mel Bartholomew recommended keeping a bucket right by the box, with a cup that you could dip in the bucket and water each square as necessary.) Weeding is easy and, as long as you check at least every couple of days, you shouldn't ever have to pull more than one or two weeds at most. Usually you won't find any because you created the soil without weed seeds.

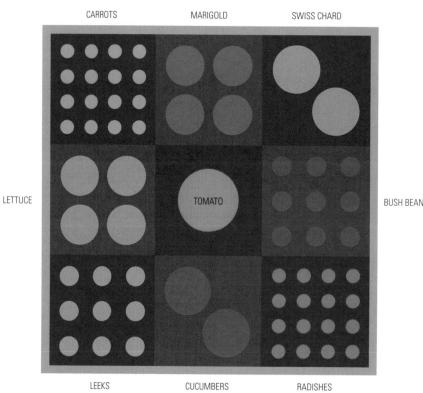

CARROTS   MARIGOLD   SWISS CHARD

LETTUCE   TOMATO   BUSH BEANS

LEEKS   CUCUMBERS   RADISHES

PLANT	PER SQUARE	PLANT	PER SQUARE
Arugula	16	Lettuce (head)	4
Basil	2	Lettuce (leaf)	16
Bean (bush)	9	Melon	1 per 2 squares
Bean (pole)	8	Okra	1
Beet	9	Onion (yellow/red/white)	16
Bok Choi	1	Oregano	1
Broccoli	1	Parsley	4
Brussels Sprout	1	Parsnip	9
Cabbage	1	Peas	8
Carrot	16	Pepper	1
Cauliflower	1	Radish	16
Celery	2	Rosemary	1
Chives	16	Rutabaga	4
Cilantro	1	Sage	1
Corn	4	Spinach	9
Cucumber	2	Strawberry	4
Dill	9	Summer Squash (vine)	1 per 2 squares
Eggplant	1	Swiss Chard	4
Fennel	2	Thyme	2
Garlic	4	Tomato	1
Kale	2	Turnip	9
Kohlrabi	4	Winter Squash (vine)	1 per 2 squares

HOW TO MAKE A SQUARE FOOT GARDENING BOX

The process of building and planting a Square Foot Gardening box is kind of fun and doesn't require any special knowledge or tools. But it will go quicker if you ask your mom or dad (or both!) to help you.

WHAT YOU'LL NEED

MEASURING TAPE

PENCIL

HANDSAW OR CIRCULAR SAW (ADULTS ONLY)

POWER DRILL AND BITS

CARPENTER'S LEVEL

2 × 6 PINE

LANDSCAPE FABRIC

$5/16$- × 1½-INCH LATH

3-INCH DECK SCREWS

2-INCH DECK SCREWS

#10-24 × 1-INCH BOLTS AND NUTS

CUT LIST

(4) 3½ × 5½ × 36-INCH PINE SIDES

(4) $5/16$ × 1½ × 37½-INCH WOOD LATH GRID

SIDES

LATH GRID

36"   37½"

TOP VIEW

1 Use a handsaw to cut four 2 × 6 boards 36 inches (95 cm) long. This will be even easier and faster if you ask your mom or dad to cut the boards with a circular saw or table saw. Choose a location for the Square Foot Garden (SFG). Clear and level the ground.

2 Place 1 board held on edge, perpendicular at the end of a board laying on its face. Mark the width of the board along the end of the board with a pencil. Repeat for all 4 boards. Stack and align the boards perfectly.

3 Mark 3 pilot hole locations centered between the board end and the marked line on a board. (The holes should also be spaced out equally side to side.) Use a drill with a ⅛-inch (.3-cm) bit to drill pilot holes at each mark, all the way down through the top 2 boards.

4 Repeat the process with the bottom 2 boards, making sure they are on dirt or on top of a waste piece of wood so you don't hit concrete when you drill through the second, bottom board.

5 Screw the boards together in overlapping joints. Use three 3-inch deck screws at each joint, driving them into the predrilled pilot holes.

Optional: if you want to make the box totally portable or appropriate for tabletop use, add a plywood bottom. Have an adult or the lumberyard or home improvement center cut a piece of ½-inch (1.3-cm) plywood to match the dimensions of the box. Place it on top of the box frame and drill pilot holes every 4 inches (10 cm) around the outside of the plywood, down into the frame. Screw the bottom to the frame with 2-inch (5-cm) deck screws. Measure, mark, and drill ¼-inch (.6-cm) drainage holes in the center of each square.

6 Place the box in position and check it for level. Remove the soil on one or more sides until the box is level both ways. Place weed-blocking landscape fabric in the bottom of the box.

7

7 Make the SFG soil mix. Measure equal amounts of vermiculite, compost, and peat moss (or, for a more environmentally friendly option, use coir) *by volume*. The easiest way to do this is to use a 5-gallon bucket and fill it with one ingredient at a time. Dump the ingredients in a mound a large tarp and use your hands to blend the mix, or ask a helper to hold one side of the tarp while you hold the other, and mix it by lifting the tarp and rolling the mixture until it's completely blended. Add the SFG mix to the box.

8 Measure and mark the sides of the box for squares both ways. Use a handsaw to cut each piece of lath 37½ inches (95 cm) long. Lay the lath in the grid lined up with the marks on the box sides. Drill 7/32-inch holes at the intersections of the lath (where they overlap) and secure those points with bolts and nuts. Screw one end of the lath down to each side of the box. As an option, you can paint the box, but make sure no paint gets inside the box. You can also paint the lath before you install it. But, again, only paint the top. No dried paint should get into the soil.

9 Plant each square in grids according to the recommended spacing for the plants you're growing (see the table on page 109).

8

HOW TO MAKE EASY PLANT MARKERS

Plant markers are a good way to know at a glance what's planted in each square of your SFG box so that you can keep a close eye on the plants and ensure they are growing as they should. There are lots of ways to make plant markers, but here's a quick and easy way.

1 Collect 9 stir sticks, which are free at local hardware stores or home improvement centers. Your mom or dad may even have extras in the garage or garden shed.

2 Cut each stick to about 4 inches (10 cm) long using a utility knife, a hacksaw, or a handsaw (be very careful and only cut *away* from your body). Cut the cut end into a point.

3 Paint or use markers to create a label with the name of what you planted in the square. This is your chance to decorate the box and provide a fun look to it, so be creative!

GO VERTICAL WITH A VEGETABLE BED

There are many advantages to vertical gardening (which is growing plants *up* rather than out). Although not all garden vegetables can be grown on vertically, the ones that can will usually thrive growing up. In exchange for a little bit of work, you'll be saving a lot of space and getting the best harvest possible.

A lot of gardeners have to deal with a small garden area, which can be a real challenge. Growing vertically can increase available growing space by as much as half.

Even if space isn't a consideration, growing vertically can be appealing for other reasons. Keep vegetables such as cucumbers or even pumpkins off the ground means you avoid flat spots, rot, and misshapen fruit. You also make your crop easier to tend and harvest—most of the time you won't even have to bend over to pick mature vegetables.

An even more important benefit is plant health. Grow vertically and you increase the air circulation around the growing plant. That, in turn, limits diseases and cuts down on pests, making them much more exposed and putting vegetables out of reach of many creepy crawlies. No matter why you choose to grow vertically, you'll need a surface on which to grow.

TYPES OF VERTICAL SUPPORTS

Growing vertically means you'll need to support the plants on a structure they can intertwine with or be tied to. There are *lots* of options.

Fence: A basic chain-link fence can be just about perfect as a vertical growing surface. The large gaps in the fence wire allow plenty of air circulation and sunlight exposure.

It's easy to twine or tie plant stems and tendrils through the fence, and chain-link fences can support a lot of weight. You can also use the south-facing surface of a board fence by stringing it with twine, wire, or some other growing supports.

Teepee: This is a tried-and-true way of growing vegetables upward. Poles (which can be bamboo, old tool handles, branches, or even curtain rods) are tied together at the top to form a pyramidal shape. Wire or twine is wrapped around the form, offering plants a 360-degree exposure

(they often grow toward their preferred light exposure). The teepee shape is widest at the bottom where the plant will be the bushiest and grow the most foliage.

A-frame: Also called a sandwich-board trellis, the A-frame offers most of the advantages of a teepee with increased air circulation. A-frames are typically more stable and easier to build than a teepee, and they are also portable, so you can use them in different areas of the garden season to season. They are made by building two rectangular frames that are joined at the top with hinges and have a body of wire mesh or twine. The frame is oriented to the north and south; shade-tolerarant plants are trained to the northern exposure and heat-loving types are grown on the opposite side.

Posts and wire: A great option where the gardener grows a vertical crop each year, this is simply supporting posts (they can be wood or metal poles) secured in the ground with wires or twine or wound between them. They can be as simple as two posts, or may be many posts that run along the entire side of the garden. The growing surface should face south and the surface should be high enough to accommodate the most vigorous climbers that will be cultivated (otherwise, the vines will start to flop over late in the season and defeat the purpose).

Structures: Many garden structures, such as gazebos, arbors, arches, and more, can be used as trellises. They usually offer a lot of growing space but, depending on the structure, may not be the best for air circulation or ease of harvesting.

Pyramid trellises offer a more orderly alternative to a teepee. As with a teepee, it's easy to train plants up all four sides of the structure, according to the sun exposure each plant prefers.

THE 5 BEST VEGETABLES FOR VERTICAL GARDENING (AND 1 FRUIT!)

Pole beans: Naturally great climbers, pole beans thrive when grown vertically. Both beans and peas grow "tendrils" from their vines, which will naturally wrap around twine, netting, or wire.

Peas: As with crops like cucumber and squash, the weight of a fully stocked pea vine—filled with mature fruit—is a consideration in growing vertical. Secure vines in place to guarantee that the plant doesn't pull away from the support or bring the support down.

Cucumbers: The big advantage to growing cucumbers vertically is that the fruit winds up longer and straighter, and more attractive. The vines with mature cucumbers on it can be surprisingly heavy, so you'll need a strong support.

Squashes: Many different types and varieties of squash—both summer and winter—can be grown up a vertical surface. Smaller types, such as acorn squash, are the best choices because they weigh less when mature and will put less strain on the support structure. For larger squash, many gardeners use cloth "hammocks" for the individual fruits. These are a bit of work but ensure the squash don't break off before they're fully ripe, possibly damaging the fruit and the plant itself.

Tomatoes (indeterminate cultivars): Indeterminate tomato plants don't stop growing until the end of the season. That's why vertical growing can be a great option to get the most tomatoes from any plant. You'll have to tie up individual stems regularly because the plant won't naturally intertwine or hold onto the support. A full crop of mature tomatoes will also be heavy, so a strong support is essential.

Grapes: Grapes are ideal for vertical gardening. They thrive when tied to a trellis or other support and are easier to pick this way.

HOW TO BUILD
AN A-FRAME TRELLIS

Also called a "sandwich board" trellis, an A-frame offers a lot of vertical area in a small footprint, which makes it ideal for space-challenged gardens. This one is easy to build and strong enough to hold a full load of mature fruit and thickly twining vines.

WHAT YOU'LL NEED

MEASURING TAPE

PENCIL

FRAMING SQUARE OR RULER

MITER HANDSAW OR MITER SAW (ADULTS ONLY)

WIRE CLIPPERS

1 × 4-INCH × 6-FOOT PINE BOARDS

1½-INCH STAINLESS STEEL WOOD SCREWS

WELDED WIRE OR CHICKEN WIRE FENCING

STAPLE GUN AND STAPLES

(2) 4-INCH (10-CM) ZINC-PLATED UTILITY HINGES

CUT LIST

(4) ¾ × 3½ × 60-INCH PINE STILES

(4) ¾ × 3½ × 48-INCH PINE RAILS

(4) ¾ × 3½ × 10-INCH PINE FEET

48 × 55-INCH WELDED WIRE OR CHICKEN WIRE PANEL

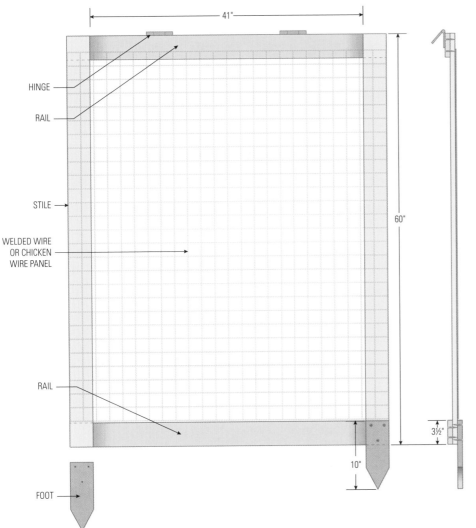

HINGE

RAIL

STILE

WELDED WIRE OR CHICKEN WIRE PANEL

RAIL

FOOT

41"

60"

3½"

10"

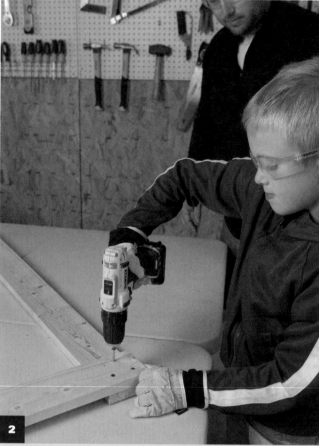

1 Make sure you have enough room to spread out on a work surface. Use a handsaw to cut the pine boards to the lengths listed on the cut list. Use wire cutters to cut the welded wire or chicken wire fencing to the dimensions on the cut list.

2 On a long, flat, level work surface, lay the two long stiles parallel to each other and 48 inches (122 cm) apart. Lay a rail at either end, overlapping the ends of the stiles and aligned with the edges. Drill pilot holes and then screw the pieces together using three 1½-inch (3.5-cm) stainless steel screws at each joint. (Have your mom or dad drill the holes if you're not allowed to use a power drill or don't feel comfortable using one.) Repeat with the remaining boards to create the second frame.

3 Use a framing square or ruler to mark identical sharp points on one end of all the 10-inch (25 cm) pine feet boards. Use a handsaw to cut the points on the feet. Screw the feet to one end of each frame, on the opposite side from the rails, using 1½-inch (3.8 cm) screws. (The top of the feet should be even with the top edge of the rail on the opposite side.)

4 Lay one frame flat on the work surface or ground, with the rails underneath. Place the wire mesh panel in position on the front of the frame so that it is centered side to side and its bottom edge is butted to the top of the feet. Staple it in place with a staple every few inches all around. Repeat with the second frame.

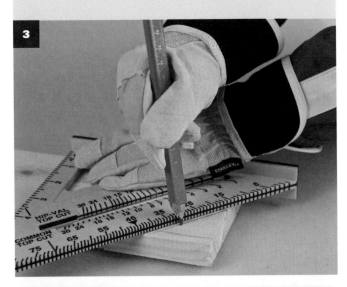

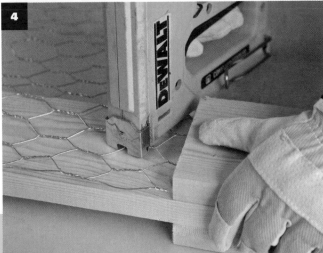

5 Lay the frames on the flat work surface with the wire mesh facing down, and the frame tops butted together. Measure and mark 12 inches (30 cm) in from each side. Align the edge of each hinge on these marks and screw the hinges in place, first on one frame, then on the opposite frame.

6 Place the trellis in the garden. The stake feet should be easy to force down into freshly turned soil, but if you have difficulty doing that, tap the top of the feet lightly with a hammer to secure the trellis in place. Tie the growing vines to the mesh panels or weave the vines in and out of the openings in the mesh (depending on the type of plant you're growing).

PLANT A TIERED HERB GARDEN TOWER

This project takes the idea of a raised bed one step further—adding levels of raised beds on top of a base layer. This makes a lot of sense for growing a range of different herbs, because some herbs have different cultivation needs from others.

Using the same principles of a time-tested construction called an "herb spiral," this tiered garden is built so that plants that prefer a drier, hotter location (such as rosemary) can be placed on the top tier, which drains much more quickly and receives more sun than lower tiers. The bottom tiers are left for herbs that can tolerate more shade and prefer moister soil.

This is also a way to grow a whole kitchen's worth of herbs in one small space. That makes a tiered raised bed a great alternative for a space-challenged gardener, because this all-in-one option can even be grown on a concrete patio—just add landscape fabric to the bottom tier to keep the soil from washing away. In any case, it will make growing, watering, tending, and harvesting your herbs easier and more pleasant. And it looks nice as well!

WHAT YOU'LL NEED

MEASURING TAPE

BRICKS, LARGE STONES, OR PAVERS

GARDEN SPADE

LEVEL

TROWEL

RAKE

HERB PLANTS

The project described here is a variation of the traditional and time-tested herb spiral. Herb spirals, like this one, are a bit of a challenge to build; an herb tower is much easier but offers the same benefits.

1. Decide where you want to put the herb garden. You need a circle of space 6 feet (1.8 m) wide in a full-sun area of the yard. Clear the ground in the location and level the soil. Spread landscape fabric, multiple layers of wet newspaper, or even cardboard over the area. Cover the fabric or cardboard with a thin layer of sand or compost.

2. Drive a stake, pole, branch, or piece of pointed wood into the center of the area you just prepared. Tie a string to it and tie the other end to a thin board or branch, so that there is 3 feet (.9 meter) of string separating the two. With the string taut, drag the outer wood piece or branch to mark a circle around the center. Remove the string and outer stick.

3. Place the first ring of bricks, stones, or pavers around the outer, marked circle. The bricks should be placed so that they are pointing toward the center (side to side, rather than end to end with one another). Push down on each and try to make it the same level as the one next to it and bed it firmly in the soil. (This may be a little difficult if you're using irregular items like stones but try your best.) If you're using bricks, check the circle with a level as you work.

4. Place a second ring of bricks on top of the first. The second layer of bricks should overlap the joints between the bricks below. When you've completed the second level, tamp down soil or sand into the joints, and walk on the brick circle several rounds to make sure the bricks are firmly secured in place.

7 Lay a second brick wall in the same way you did the first, along the second, smaller circle. Make sure the bricks are firmly bedded down in the soil, and fill the circle with potting soil or topsoil as before. Nestle a terracotta or other plant pot in the center of the second circle, and fill with soil. Plant your herbs to fill the different levels.

5 Fill inside the brick circle with potting or topsoil. Rake it out level. Spray the soil with water just so that it is moist, but not soaking wet.

6 Tie the string to the stake once again, shortening it so that is 18 inches (46 cm) long. Tie the second stick to the outside of the string and scribe a circle 3 feet (.9 meter) in diameter on the soil you just added. Remove the stakes and string.

INDEX